Holl
By Mark Kurtis Jr.

HOLLER HOUSE

First edition. March 15, 2021.

Copyright © 2021 Mark Kurtis Jr.

ISBN: 978-1393989134

Written by Mark Kurtis Jr.

Table of Contents

This book is dedicated to my friend, and brother, Angel. A man who was taken far too soon, but managed to touch the hearts and minds of all those who knew him.

With love and Respect, Bro...

Angel Rodriguez

September 8, 1984-

December 31, 2020

I base the following story on true events.
I have changed the names to protect those who were fortunate enough to survive.
I feel they've suffered enough... don't you?

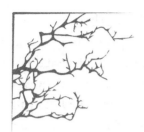

Prologue

No one wanted to get that call in the early morning hours telling you a family member or a loved one was hurt. I believe it magnifies the experience greatly when that person is your own child. Unfortunately, this was exactly the situation my father found himself in on that wintry day in December 2001, just as the sun ushered in a new day.

I was on my way home from taking my mother, June, to work at the nursing home. Our family only had one vehicle at this point and we all had jobs we needed to get to, so it was share and share alike. It was frustrating being a teen with a license and no car of my own. Most of my friends had their own wheels, and I was very jealous of them. This was why I found myself on one of Pennsylvania's notorious, winding back roads on a frosty winter morning.

I don't recall a lot of what happened, but what little I do sometimes still haunts me. I was coming around a blind curve and there was black ice on the road. For those people who don't realize what black ice is, count your blessings. What makes it so treacherous is you can't see it at night until it's too late, and in a blink of an eye it changes your life. I still recall as the car slid into the oncoming lane and all I saw were headlights. I would wake up in a cold sweat for the next year as I dreamed of those bright beams.

The next memory I had was crawling from the wreck that was once my father's 1988 Oldsmobile. I had flashes of seeing the other driver as he held his arm in pain and asked him if he was alright. I then sat down beside a tree and wiped the sweat off my face. I found out later it wasn't sweat but blood. The paramedics got to the scene and the following hours of my life are a blur. My father was asking the doctors to clean me up a bit before letting my mother see me. Pop would later say I looked horrible.

"Joe, your head went into the windshield and then the side of your head broke the driver's side window. Your nose was so broken it was on the right side of your face and it swelled your right eye shut,". He always adds at the end of his tale how he immediately vomited after receiving the phone call from the police. I can only imagine the horror a phone call like that would bring to a loving parent.

I wasn't wearing my seat belt, and I realize in some circumstances the seatbelt can do more harm than good, but this was not one of them. If I'd been wearing it, I wouldn't have lost my top teeth and severely injured my bottom teeth and my face. I think I was the only kid at prom that year with dentures!

Pop had them transfer me because he wasn't at all confident in the treatment I was getting in the first hospital's trauma unit. Before they transferred me I was holding my Father's hand,

"Pop, sorry about the car," I blurted out in a heavy daze.

"Oh my God, Joe, don't worry about the damn car. We'll see you when you get to the other hospital," he was fighting back tears. Mom later told me she had to drive while they followed me to the other hospital because Pop was crying too hard. My mother would shed her tears for me later.

The next thing I recall is waking up to pee in a plastic jug. The doctors needed a urine specimen and if I couldn't wake up and provide one, they'd have to use a catheter. I was already having a bad day. So in front of my family, friends, and nursing staff, I whipped it out and gave them a sample. I remember hearing laughter through what were obvious tears. I was in the hospital living off of milkshakes and soft foods with my jaw wired shut for the better part of three weeks. To top all this off, my parents had given me a beautiful leather jacket for Christmas and I was wearing it during the accident. The paramedics had to cut it off of me at the hospital. It was one of the best presents I ever got, and I could only enjoy it for such a short time.

My parents and siblings came to see me as often as they could and when they weren't there one or more of my friends would come. The boss even confronted my Father about missing so much time. Pop informed him not to make him choose between his kid and his job. His boss wouldn't like the answer. Even though my Father's income was essential to our survival, he felt his children were more important. Mom and Dad hated seeing me in that bed, and they really didn't enjoy leaving me every night.

Although I was in agony and while I was lucky to be alive, I didn't feel very lucky. My face was hamburger, and I wasn't exactly beating the girls off with a stick before the accident. I didn't think anyone would want to be with me now that I lost my teeth and had a bent nose (even after two surgeries). I would also carry scars for the rest of my life. Upon retrospect, I know I am fortunate enough to be alive. If you could see the car, you'd know I easily could have died.

New Year's Eve was very tough that year. My family usually threw a big party to bring in the new year and the although my parents didn't feel it was appropriate, my brother and sister convinced them to have the party to bring everyone's spirits up. I also told them to throw the party. I didn't want to ruin everyone's good time. Besides, it introduced me to Demerol that night and it was amazing. I was feeling no pain that night while I watched old sitcoms and laughed till I eventually passed out. The party was not the uplifting experience everyone thought it would be. Most of the people at the party were crying and wishing I was there. The alcohol didn't help. Once my friends and family had a few, the tears flowed. I heard all about it when I finally got released and went home. Odd as it may seem, hearing all this made me feel better.

I felt so loved by those around me and it was their support and love which helped me get through such a trying time. It was my senior year of high school, which is to be the best one, and I was out of school for over a month. The rumors were flying around too. People were saying I was driving drunk, and that's what caused the accident. My friends defended me in my absence with the truth of what happened. My recovery was slow going, and I was dealing with the aftermath of the accident. I was getting terrible migraines and to this day I still get them. To top it all off, the guy in the SUV I hit was suing me!

My injuries were so severe; I was in the hospital for almost a month. My family lost money and the only vehicle we had, and I was living with pain every day. This guy lost his Ford Explorer and bruised his elbow, and he was suing me. I guess I get it. It was my fault on all accounts, it just bothered me.

The reason I'm telling you all this is very simple. If there was ever a time I needed my family to pull together, it was then and pull together they did. They wrapped me up in a protective cocoon after the accident. Mom and Pop took incredible care of me when I finally got home, and when they weren't there, my brother and sister helped me. If I ever had any doubts about whether they loved or valued me, they were quickly extinguished. The Hunters knew how to deal with adversity, and if I may say so, we kicked its ass. Our strength as a unit was incredible and a few years following the accident, that strength got tested to the extreme. Whatever you take away from reading this account, please believe when I say family was and is my strength.

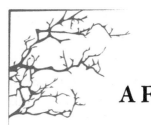

A FRESH START

We needed to get out of our old neighborhood. It was once an area where low-income parents could raise their children and send them to a decent public school, away from the city. Those days were now in the past. The new people who were moving into the neighborhood were not the kinds of folks my parents wanted my siblings and me associating with. My family and I watched as the good people we'd known for years, left for greener pastures and their homes became drug dens. Before we moved out, two of those houses were synonymous with crack heads and meth users.

My father was so excited when he and mom found the place. It wasn't very far from where we were living. It was just far enough and just secluded enough; anyone wouldn't bother us. Over the years, my dad became disenchanted by people. His cynicism grew with each passing conversation he had with his neighbors. People looked to him as the community leader, and I believe that fed into his ego. He always enjoyed helping people when he could. However, when the time came when we needed the help, most people did their very best Houdini impression and vanished.

If we moved into the new house, my sister could still attend the same high school and graduate just like her two brothers. My brother James and I were already out of school and working full time. We were both still living at home, not wanting to face the world without mommy and daddy. Why would we move out when our parents took care of so well? I was working at the local big box store in town and my brother was doing his best to break into modeling and acting.

I knew I never had a face for the big screen and the only modeling gig I could ever get was the before pics in a weight loss commercial. I turned my attentions to my friends and girls. My friends and I were close and the girl would come into my life after we moved into the new house. Back then, I thought writing for a living was a pipe dream. Still, I could spin a good yarn now and then.

We were a happy family. If you read this and come away with nothing else, please believe we were a happy family. We were nowhere near rich, but my mom and dad did all they could do to see us raised right. They made an honest living off the sweat of their brows and never hung their heads in shame. I still admire them for it. The three of us kids were very close to our parents, which is why the next five months were so brutal. My family all but tore itself apart living in that Godforsaken house. I realize this is a cliché, but we really believed we found our home when we first saw it. None of us could fathom the hell that awaited us when mom and dad signed the lease.

It was a Saturday morning on a bitter December day. I just got home from a night of teenage debauchery with my friends when I walked in the door. My father was already up and about drinking his coffee; he was in an especially jovial mood.

"Hey bubba, are you just getting in?" he asked, knowing full well I was.

I nodded, hung over. I'm not a morning person and probably will never be one. My dad was the exact opposite. When the sun came up he was up, as if the rays had rejuvenated him. He was also loud when he spoke and intentionally turned up the volume when he knew I'd been drinking.

"Don't get cozy, we have places to go," he sipped at his black Folgers. I've never been one for coffee, and not that bitter brew Pop would drink.

"No Pop, I'm burned out. I'm just gonna crash for a while," I pleaded.

Pop's eyes narrowed; even though I was technically an adult by the state's standards, to him I was still a boy. To this day, if the man gave me the right look, I'd sit down. It wasn't out of fear, but respect.

"Boy, you're going with us; I want you there so I can get your opinion on the house. Your mother and I think this could be the one that gets us out of this place."

"'The house', you mean to say we finally found a place within our price range, and it doesn't suck? Where is it? Please tell me it's still in town?"

"I can't say it doesn't suck until I see it with my own eyes, but I know the house and the land it's on is beautiful. To answer your other question, yes, it is in town. It's right around the damn corner from here."

The pounding in my head was subsiding. A feeling of elation was sweeping over me. My parents were lifelong renters. Mom and Pop's credit was not the best, and no bank in America would ever give them a mortgage. The housing bubble was not a thing yet. They were living paycheck to paycheck, so they needed something on the lower end, which also could house three grown children. It wasn't an ideal situation, but we were going to make it work.

"Where is this place?" I asked while downing two Advil.

"You know the dam?" Pop replied.

"Are you talking about Angora Lake? Pop the houses around there are way out of our price range. We couldn't even afford to trick or treat there as kids."

"Shut up, you make it sound like we're destitute," Pop's pride was ever present, "Besides, I'm not talking about those snobs on the hill. I'm talking about the house down in the Angora Holler. The big white one downstream from the dam."

I thought about the area he was referring to and it just wasn't clicking. The big white house in front of the dam? There weren't any houses in front of the dam. The next building after the dam was the old Bixby Lodge, a local bar.

"I'm not sure where you mean Pop? Is it down past Bixby's?"

"No Bubba, look here," he placed the butter dish in the middle of the table, "here's the dam," he then placed the salt shaker away from it, "here is Bixby's and here we are."

He placed the pepper shaker in between the butter and the salt. The granulated black and gray in the shaker should have been a warning of the darkness to come.

"Pop, the only building in the holler is the old mill."

"Right, that's the house. The converted building was now a split family home. We'd be on the side facing Bixby's."

"Great, so when that old dam breaks, we won't see the water coming for us. Hilarious Pop, but I'm going to sleep. No one lives in that rundown shack. Who are you trying to kid?"

"Why must you have such a negative attitude, boy? Your mother will be down in a few minutes and she's very excited about this. I don't want you to ruin this for her. You understand Joe?"

I was in utter disbelief. My father was being serious. How in the hell could anyone live in that building? Anyone who lived in such a place would worry incessantly about the dam bursting and the raging flood waters obliterating life as they knew it. Or maybe that was just me. A few years prior to these events, a hurricane swept through the northeast and the rain hammered us for days. Rumors were flying around the neighborhood that the dam would burst and Angora Lake would flood the town. The devastation would've been massive, but whether by fate or by luck, the dam held.

My mother all but danced into the kitchen and she too was in a good mood for the time of day. Mom was also not a morning person, but on that chilly morning she exuded joy. She couldn't wait to see this house.

"Did Pop tell you the splendid news?" she said, making herself a cup of tea.

I nodded, still trying to shake off the effects of one too many.

"The four of us are heading out in fifteen minutes, so be ready," Pop finished his first cup of coffee and poured a second. He needed at least half a pot in him.

"Four? Where is James? Why doesn't he have to go to this family outing?" I was jealous; all I wanted to do was sleep.

"You know he works third shift and needs his sleep. Don't worry about James; we'll give him a full report when we get home," Pop explained.

My brother worked in the local tire shop's warehouse overnight. During the day, he'd be on the phone with perspective agents or trying to get into the next available acting class. James was the consummate dreamer.

My sister was the last one down the stairs. Marie slowly slogged into the kitchen, dressed and ready to face the bitter Pennsylvania cold. Her long brown hair brushed to perfection and brown eyes still glazed over with sleep residue. She poured herself a cup of coffee and sipped at it quietly. I whispered to her so Mom and Pop wouldn't hear, "Did they tell you where the house is?"

"Yeah, Joey, we're just going to look at it. We set nothing in stone," she responded, clearing her throat. She was the only one in the family who called me Joey. She was almost a full grown woman by this point and still refused to call me Joe, and on the rare occasion she tried, it came out awkward. I enjoyed her still calling me Joey. Somehow, it reminded me she would always be my little sister.

The four of us piled into our gold Saturn coup, which was still warming up, and my family put that thing through the ringer. It wasn't the best vehicle, but you couldn't kill it. It started faithfully every morning. We left the old neighborhood and traveled down Butler Lane road. We'd been down this stretch countless times over the years, but this time there was a small sense of hope in me. Maybe Pop's excitement over the place was a good thing? Maybe it was the perfect house for us and we would finally be out of the old place. We turned and were now parallel with the Pebble Creek; the stream coming from Angora Lake became Pebble Creek once you got past Bixby's Lodge.

Pebble Creek was a fond memory of my childhood. My friends and I would walk down Butler with buckets in our hands and try to catch crayfish under the watery rocks. Some days we were there for hours. Also, the local public swimming pool was nearby and Mom and Pop would scrape together enough money to buy a family membership over the summer. Pop never joined us at the pool, he was usually working, and he hated public pools. The man had seen Caddy Shack one too many times and believed people used pools as bathrooms.

We rounded the bend leading to the dam, and I still caught no sight of the house. A person had trouble seeing the place from the road. Especially in summer, when the trees were in full bloom, and their branches stretched out in full splendor. Pop put on his left turn signal and we turned down a long and winding driveway leading to the place. My father was not wrong about the surrounding land. It was right out of a fairy tale book. Between the flowing waters from the dam and the lush green, forest like setting, it was picturesque. One would think Hansel and Gretel would lay breadcrumbs down somewhere near.

The house sat right in front of the side of a mountain and a path led from the building right down to Bixby's. A small bridge went from the driveway across the water near the main road. Pop parked the car on the bridge. After we moved in this would be my parking space, even though my father frowned on it. He wasn't a fan of me blocking the bridge.

The land may have been gorgeous, but the house was not. The structure saw better days in its time. The white paint was chipping off, and the windows seemed to leer at you. As if the house was sizing you up for a meal. The panes of glass that were still intact needed a good scrubbing. That hadn't happened since they built the place. The place oozed with gloom and a sense of dread. The dilapidated front porch and many of the old floorboards were broke or were reaching their breaking point. Tree roots lined the front yard leading to the porch. If you were not careful, you could easily trip and fall over them. They were sticking out of the ground all around. Pop once commented it was part of the land's charm. All it would take was a sprained ankle and the charm would dissipate.

We all got out of the car and my sister and I shared a glance. We didn't need any words. We were both thinking the same thing, *what a dump.* Pop was focusing on the land itself. It was as if he never even noticed the house. I watched him take a deep breath of winter air and step off the bridge. In his mind, he could see all the different projects he could accomplish. He was surveying the land when the front door opened with a loud creak. The hinges were as old as the house was from the horrendous groan they made. Out stepped this very elderly woman. Judging from her age, she had been born right around the time God said "let there be light". She needed a cane to get around and her body resembled a question mark. Her jowls hung so low I was afraid she'd trip on them. An image of Droopy Dog came to mind the first time I saw her.

"Are you Joe Hunter?" her voice sounded worse than the hinges did.

Pop quickly spun around and faced her. The voice brought him back to reality from the natural beauty around him.

"Yes mam I am, Joe Hunter Sr. This is my wife June, my son Joe Jr., and my daughter Marie. Are you the woman I spoke to on the phone yesterday?"

"That's right, are you still interested in the place?" There was a hint of surprise that we'd shown up at all.

I was astonished she didn't kill herself on the rickety steps. For a woman of advanced years, she still got around, but slowly.

"Well, we'd like to see it first," Pop replied, "Before we commit to anything."

"The current tenants have been fixing the place up while they've been living here. They're in the house now in fact if you'd like to meet them?"

As if on cue, a middle age man with a tie-dye shirt burst out of the screen door, his hair pulled back into a ponytail. The man was a flower child if I ever saw one.

"Virginia is everything alright?" he asked.

"Yes, Roger, these people are here to inquire about the house. This is Joe and his wife June," Virginia responded, attempting to make her way back up the steps to the door.

Roger gave my father a quick look and smiled. He shook my dad's hand and grimaced as Pop showed his grip. Pop loved to crush hands when he shook them, and if you didn't know it was coming, it could hurt.

"Can I offer you a drink of wheatgrass? It's fantastic in the morning," Roger said.

"No thanks, I've got my coffee," Pop gave me an amused look, as if he'd ever put anything like that in his body.

One of the first things I noticed was the extensive amount of spider webs all over the porch. They were everywhere, but being December the inhabitants of those webs were long dead. However, new ones would be around come spring. Our family didn't do well with spiders.

Walking through the front door, the smell of the old place hit you first. The house had an earthy aroma, musty with and a bit of mold. Right as you entered, the steps leading up to the second floor were directly in front of you, and I remember them being narrow. The surrounding walls had that unfinished surface that could scratch the hell out of you if you weren't careful. To your left was the kitchen and dining area. Mom loved how big the kitchen was and commented on it having an electric stove. To the right of the steps was the living room. It was smaller than the kitchen, but we could get our furniture in there. In back of the staircase, there were the steps leading down to the basement. A door separated the entrance from the living room and the kitchen. It was odd to have two entries to the basement, it just always seemed strange to me. That was the first floor.

The joy in my father's eyes when he saw the land for the first time was in stark contrast to the expression I saw on his face now. He was not at all impressed with the inside of the house. My mother and sister seemed to follow his lead. The architecture bothered me. The layout of the first floor just made little sense to me.

"How old is this house, Ginny?" Pop asked as he knocked on one of the kitchen walls.

"Well, they built it in 1792 by an ironmaster. When it changed hands, it became a paper mill and then a wool mill. My family acquired it in 1860 and please call me Virginia."

"Lot of history here, eh boy," Pop nudged my rib cage. While it was true, I had a love for history of all kinds, I was kind of preoccupied by the small window in the kitchen. It was very close to the refrigerator and much like the door next to the basement, it just didn't belong there. The set up was just wrong to me.

"Why is that window there, Virginia?" my curiosity got the better of me.

It made her uncomfortable for one so young to use her first name.

"Oh, well, so your mother there can have a magnificent view when she's in here cooking."

"A view of what, the side of the mountain?" Marie spoke up, and she wasn't wrong. The window just offered a view of about two feet from the house to the mountainside. It was the worst potential spot for a window.

The next part of our tour took us to the second floor and the confusing layout continued. From the steps to your right was the master bedroom, which would become Mom and Pop's room. To the left was a nice size room my sister would soon sleep in. This room was the only room with a bathroom in it, and we had to go through my sister's room to use it. I'm sure it was maddening for her. A teenage girl to have so little privacy, but she made do.

The bathroom was not pleasant. The paint on the walls looked to be from 1970. It was a drab mint green color. My father always thought bathrooms should be white. White meant clean. A pungent odor always emanated from the bathroom. Also, it was tiny. If two people were in there, they cramped it.

Our future landlord stayed downstairs while we looked over the two top floors. Her limited mobility did not lend itself to such steep stairs. While Mom and Marie were looking over the master room, Pop and I were inspecting the bathroom.

"What do you think, bubba?"

"To be honest Pop, I really don't like the layout of the house. What the hell was the architect on when he drew up these plans?"

Pop rubbed his beard in thought for a moment.

"It was 1792 they originally designed the place as a mill, not a house. Maybe the builder thought no one would ever live here? C'mon let's head up to the attic and see what's what."

The staircase leading up to the attic was exactly like the others, very narrow and very steep. Again there were two doorways like the ones connecting my sister's room to my parents' room, but only one lone door (the other was long gone). The door was next to the third floor stairs. I realize I keep going on about the layout of this place, but it can't be overstated how odd it was. Once we were at the top the two rooms broke off to the left and the right. Both rooms were in horrible disrepair. Horrible sky blue paint was chipping off the walls. The room I would turn into my poker room had a busted window. If the current tenants were indeed fixing the joint up for Virginia, there wasn't a lot of evidence of it. The other bedroom was to be James' room, but he seldom was in it. James and I took to sleeping down in the living room for reasons I will get into later. In short, the place was a dive. It wasn't fit for the rodents in the walls, let alone human beings.

The four of us were standing in the kitchen with Virginia after we finished looking over the basement. Pop was nervous because the house ran on oil heat and we never had to worry about oil before. Virginia did her best to put his mind at ease.

"If you move in by the beginning of next month, there will be plenty of oil in there," she promised.

"And you say you only want six hundred a month for the place?" Pop was ready to leave right then if she asked for one more cent.

"That's right. It's a grand house for a family. Why, there is a nice family just on the other side of you, and I hear no complaints from them. What do you think, Joe?"

Mom stared at Pop, and I knew this was the best we could hope for at that point in our lives. My parents wanted out of the housing development we were currently living in, and they knew they didn't have a lot of money. Pop's courier business was still getting off the ground, and Mom was still working part time in the nursing home kitchen. For Christ's sake, the two of them didn't even have health insurance.

"What do you think, June?" asked Pop, placing a loving arm around her.

"I think we can make this a home for us. Besides, you love the land. Think of all we could do with the land out there," my mother was making the best of the situation. "Also, Marie can stay in the same school and graduate. I think we can make this work."

I told them since I was still living at home I would chip in and help where I could. Oil heat is not cheap, and it would be a cold winter in a house this big. If we only knew how cold it would get in that house. I am positive beyond any doubt, if Mom and Pop Hunter had any inkling what the next five months would bring, they would've politely told the old woman 'thank you for your time' and left. As it is, they signed a six-month agreement. It might as well have been a pact with the devil himself. I guess hindsight really is twenty/twenty.

WE PICKED A HELL
OF A NIGHT

We needed to be out of our current home by the month's end. The day after we left they changed the locks, so we were right up against it- time wise. The fact it was the end of December did little to help the situation. The temperatures were to dip into the teens that day and even lower at night. A threat of snow was predicted, but the risk was low enough that we thought we could get it done before it covered the roads. Those assumptions might well have been reality if we started moving earlier in the day. Unfortunately, most of the family worked during the day so we couldn't start until late afternoon.

One of my best friends Dave offered to help us move into the new place. All he asked was for us to feed him. Dave was and still is a fantastic human being. The move was going to take us well into the night and even though he worked the next morning; he said he'd call off because we needed the help. My father wouldn't hear of him losing a day's pay to help us, so Pop paid him his day's pay. Dave tried to refuse, but my Pop could be very persuasive when need be. Years later Dave and I would tell of the moving night and the horrible experience it was.

It was freezing by the time we were loading up the U-Haul. We all tried to keep it light by cracking jokes while we cleaned out the old house in record time. Mom and Marie concentrated on the boxes and the kitchen stuff while the four men were lifting the heavy furniture and packing it all up nice and tight. Within a few hours, the house was devoid of any trace of the Hunter family. All except the eighteen years of memories we accrued. It may have been a low income home, but Mom and Pop really poured their hearts and souls into it. My mother's own childhood was not what you would call ideal, and because of circumstances beyond her control forced her to move countless times. It made making friends and concentrating on school all but impossible.

When my father and she became a couple, he promised her a stable life, even if he had to break his back to do it. It was a promise he kept to her and his back. For the better part of eighteen years we lived in the same home and we stayed in the same school. However, the years of labor were not kind to my Dad's spine. By the time that frigid December night came, his back was so bad James, Dave, and I flat out refused to let him lift anything over a lamp. We told him to supervise.

After we loaded the truck, Mom and Marie set about cleaning the place one last time. Mom did not wish to leave any excuse for the owners to come after us for leaving the place a mess. I stared at the bare walls of my childhood room. James and I shared this room for most of our lives. Pop and I played video games in that room for hours on end. The first time I got high was in that very room. The memories came flooding back, and I almost had to fight back tears.

"You ok man?" I never noticed Dave standing beside me.

"Yeah, I'm fine; it's just hitting me this is the last time I'll be in this room."

"I get it, but it's getting late, and it just started snowing. Pop wants to get going."

I nodded and unplugged the lamp. We headed down to the truck. I instantly noticed Dave was right. Old man winter was upon us, and he let loose with a vengeance.

Butler Lane Rd. was slick with a dusting of snow, as we made our way to the new house. My other friend Mike texted me and said he'd meet us at the new place and help us unload. He worked later and couldn't help until his shift was over. I noticed his car out front of the place as Pop carefully drove that long moving truck down the winding, steep, driveway. It was treacherous during the daytime in perfect weather; here we were in the dead of night during a snowstorm! Pop was a magician with driving. He negotiated every turn with precision and somehow got the back end of that behemoth facing the front porch of the new house.

The snow was coming down even harder as we unloaded. The tree roots sticking out of the ground and the slippery snow made hauling the heavier items even more cumbersome. The couch was easily the worst. I needed to climb the first few steps to the second floor so we could pivot it into the living room. I skinned my elbow against the jagged surface of the wall. It hurt like hell, but we got the couch in there.

The rest of the unloading continued at a quicker pace, primarily because the temp was plummeting. Then we still needed to use the truck to get over to my Grandmother's house and pick up the drop freezer she was giving mom. It was approaching midnight when the truck was empty and Pop, Dave, and I headed over to Nanny's house. The cab of the truck only held two people, so Dave needed to ride in the back... with a hand dolly.

"You'll be fine," Pop encouraged Dave as he stepped into the trailer.

"Just please take it easy, going around turns Pop," Dave begged.

We're still not sure who it was that secured the dolly, but going around one turn it broke free and nearly killed Dave. We heard a tirade of curses and screams as Dave dodged the hand truck. Looking back, it really was a stupid move. In the middle of a snowstorm going over mountain roads and having a person in the trailer with a loose dolly, someone could've really gotten hurt.

And to this day Dave has never let me forget it.

My Grandmother was her usual hypochondriac self as Dave and I struggled to get the drop freezer out of her damn basement. By this point all of us were ready for this night to be over, and we were getting very close. While the three of us were dealing with my grandmother, the rest of the family and Mike were back at the house moving furniture and trying to create a semblance of order. Once we got the freezer in the truck Pop strapped it in and made sure the dolly wasn't going anywhere again.

"There you go, Dave. That thing shouldn't move this time around," Pop said.

"Not my problem, Pop," Dave explained, "Joe is riding in the back this time. I'll be up front with you and the heat!"

I really didn't want to do it, but how could I argue with the guy? Here he was helping my family out, freezing his ass off and on top of all of that he nearly got maimed by a runaway hand truck. I got in the trailer and sat next to the freezer for some stability. The trip back was uneventful.

The snow was several inches deep when we got back. Pop crawled the moving truck over the untreated roads. We were well into the wee hours of the morning when we reached the holler. There was a certain beauty to the house and the land as the winter storm raged on. We placed the drop freezer on the only stone slab in the basement. A good portion of the place was still dirt. Dave and I were coming out of the basement and walked into Mike apologizing to Pop.

"I'm sorry Pop, I completely forgot about her. Between unloading the truck and then trying to get everything situated..."

My father waved his hand at Mike in understanding. Our family were animal lovers, and we always had pets. During this stage of our lives, we had four of them. The two dogs, Duke and Max, were a sight to behold. Duke was a mix of basset and beagle, but his appearance lent itself to more beagle. Max was one hundred percent pug, complete with a smashed in face and breathing problems. Then we had two goddamn birds. I've never been a fan of birds. You can't cuddle them and they crap all over you. These two particular winged spawns were not a credit to their species. Floyd was an African-Gray parrot who never stopped squawking... ever. The other was a small love bird, completely the antithesis of her name. This bird hated everyone. If you tried to reach in her cage, the nasty creature would attack! Its beak may not have been large, but it could hurt if it got a hold of you.

The love bird's cage was sitting on the kitchen table, and it didn't take a genius to put the case together. Pop was holding the bird in his hands and the poor thing was gasping for air. Those birds cannot handle such arctic temperatures, and in the confusion of moving, we forgot it on the front porch.

"It's ok boy, it was an honest mistake," Pop reassured Mike who was on the verge of tears.

"Maybe the vet could..." Pop's shaking head interrupted Mike.

"No, she's been out there awhile and we have to stop her suffering."

"Can the vet put her down or..."

In one swift motion, my father gave the bird one last moment of kindness. He snapped her neck and ended her pain. It killed my father to do it. He loved animals, maybe even more than humans. He did it as a mercy.

"Oh, good God!" Mike bellowed as he watched it happen. Having no love for the bird, Dave and I laughed at his response. Pop placed the bird back into her cage and put the cage back on the porch.

"So are we all in? The freezer is downstairs, are the beds set up? Can we finally get some sleep?" Pop asked.

Everyone nodded and Mike told us he really had to get going before he couldn't anymore. The weather was picking up and his car barely made it back to his house as it was. The rest of us sat in the kitchen reflecting on the day's events. We held a sense of pride in the fact we got it all done in the middle of what the weatherman said 'would only be a dusting'. How anyone could be so wrong, so frequently and still keep a job is beyond me.

We were all in the kitchen for about an hour and even with all the doors and windows shut; the house was still not warming up. Every one of us was wearing multiple layers to get warm. The heat was not coming. Pop went down to the oil tank, and the bubble was reading half full, but still no heat came. Over the next few days, we discovered the oil tank gauge was defective, and the tank was empty. Also, the radiators throughout the house were malfunctioning and not producing any heat.

We were in for a frosty night.

Mom and Pop got all bundled up and headed off to bed. Dave still talks about the way Pop looked wrapped up in a makeshift papoose. We laugh about it now, but we weren't laughing then. We all bundled up and made an attempt at sleep. I think it was only through sheer exhaustion any of us found it.

The next morning brought us a bright sunny day. Inside the house we could see our breath. I don't remember ever being so cold. I glanced outside and there was at least a foot of snow on the ground. My brother James was already hard at work trying to shovel out our cars. Dave and I were starving at this point and prepared to go out and begin digging our way out. We found out that day the snow plows didn't service our new road. It was too dangerous for the plow trucks. It was up to our landlady to get the snow removed and we were not about to wait for that. So there we were, the three of us, shoveling at least three blocks from the house to the main road. It was a daunting task, but we were keen to get out of there.

HOLLER HOUSE

James wanted to see his girlfriend and Dave and I wanted pizza. Pop was proud of how quickly we cleared a path for the cars. There was enough room for just one vehicle, but you could get out. After the shoveling we were back in the house catching our breath and it was, then my family received glorious news. My sister's boyfriend Zack and his mother heard about our issues with the heat and immediately brought over space heaters. They would run our electric bill up, but we didn't argue. There was one for every room in the house. I'll never forget the feeling as those space heaters broke the chill off the house.

Dave and I went to our local haunt for some well-deserved food and we sat there devouring every morsel. The move, and the shoveling exhausted us, so there wasn't much in the way of conversation.

"We picked a hell of a night, huh?" I chuckled as I took another bite of my slice.

"Yeah, but we got it done, bro. Just think, the worst is over," Dave's words comforted me. I only wish they were true. The events over the next few months would prove that the frozen night we spent moving into the holler house would represent some happier moments. At least during those cold hours, we still smiled and laughed.

I think back on that night with hindsight, and maybe all those things that went wrong were omens, or warnings. The bird, the heat, the oil tank, hell- even the snowstorm that dumped on us: maybe they were all signs of us not to move into that place. It's easy to look back and judge, but the Hunters never believed in taking the easy road. Somehow, someway, life always made us take the hard road.

SLOAN'S OFFERING

E xcerpt from Interview with Joe Hunter Sr.
   Joe Sr: I hated that house with a passion. I cannot overstate how much I despised that damn place from the very beginning. From day one, I started fixing things around the house that Virginia never got to.

THE SECOND DAY IN THE new house I was working and was in for quite a story when I arrived home. My father was in the middle of fixing the bathroom sink. Before I left for work that day he'd told me the former tenants never got around to fixing the leaky pipe underneath it. Pop was not a plumber by any means, but he could fix a leak here and there. He was often proud of saying, "I'm a jack of all trades but a master of none".

I heard Mom, Marie, and Pop discussing something with earnest as I opened the front door. They were in the living room and Pop was very adamant.

"I'm telling you he was there, dammit! There have to be footprints out there," Pop declared. He was pacing back and forth. He was definitely in an unnerved state of mind.

"Zack and I looked out where you said to look," Marie tried to calm him down but it was no use. "There are no foot prints in the snow."

"Don't tell me, little girl! I know what I saw and who I saw. He was there, and I watched him walk down the path to Bixby's."

My Mother gave me a confused glance and then Pop finally noticed me.

"What's going on?" I asked.

"I was upstairs fixing the damn bathroom sink when the dogs started going ballistic. You should've heard them barking and howling. You'd have thought they were losing their minds. I tried to get them to relax, but they kept freaking out. Finally, I went downstairs to see what was going on and as I walked down the steps, I see this straw hat through the window on top of the door."

Pop was visibly shaking at this point. This was not a man who scared easily. In fact, I never witnessed him take a step back from anyone in my life. Tough didn't even describe my dad. The man had taken care of himself since he was sixteen. So it was rather alarming to see him so upset.

"*Who the hell could that be?* I opened the door and there was this small man with thick seventies style mustache. He was a little guy, wearing summer overalls and no shoes!"

"Pop, there is a foot of snow out there; you're telling me he wasn't wearing any shoes?" I did not hide my sarcasm.

"That's exactly what we said, Joe," Mom replied.

"Anyway, I open the door and he smiles at me and goes, 'Hi, I know you just moved in and I thought you'd like to have this'. With this thick Dutch accent."

Pop showed me a small postcard with a black-and-white picture on it. It was a photograph of our house and the surrounding land. The edges of the picture were stained yellow with time, but it was clear as day it was our house. At first I thought nothing of it. The house was old and there's bound to be several photos of it.

"Ok, so he gave you this, I don't understand the entire hubbub?" I said.

"I took it, told him thank you, and he tipped his hat and turned and left down the path. I closed the door and went back to work, but when I got halfway up the stairs I realized he wasn't wearing any shoes. There's a foot of snow down that path and this guy is in his bare feet. I threw the door open again, and he's not there."

Pop stopped to light his Marlboro. He was so flustered he couldn't even get his Zippo to fire up. Marie did it for him.

"I sat down in my recliner and was staring at the postcard till Mom and Marie got home."

"He had me and Zack go out and check for footprints," Marie sounded irritated. "When we told him there wasn't any out here, he screamed, 'No!'. He kept saying we were missing them."

"I finally went out and checked for myself Bubba, and son of a bitch if I can't find any. It makes no sense," Pop slammed his hand on the coffee table.

The situation exhausted me from a long day of helping idiotic customers at work. The last thing I wanted to hear was a *ghost* story involving our new home. My mother who had remained quiet through most of this conversation finally chimed in, "Pop, maybe you accepted an offering."

My mother is a very superstitious woman. If she ever said something bad might happen to someone or something, she would always knock on wood. All of us were firm believers in the paranormal, but we also had a healthy dose of skepticism. Before we jumped off the deep end and blamed other worldly entities for our troubles, we looked for a more tangible cause. My mother however was one of the first to jump to a spooky conclusion.

"You remember my brother's house in the city? He found that nice candelabra and kept it instead of throwing out with the rest of the old tenant's junk. A few weeks later, all hell broke loose in that place," Mom explained. "They were told by the medium the candelabra was an offering."

Pop, Marie, and I stared blankly at her.

"Ah, go on June, what happened in George's house was a long time ago, and there were a lot of other things about that place other than the candelabra," Pop brushed her off.

"Yeah, Mom, chances are there is something that explains all of this," I said.

"Well I got to get back to that sink so here, Marie, put this somewhere. I don't have time for all this," Pop grabbed his wrench and headed back upstairs.

Mom and Marie went into the kitchen to get a jump on dinner. My curiosity got the better of me and I went outside in search of barefoot prints. I only saw three sets and Marie told me Zack, Pop, and she made those. I stood in the snow for a while, trying to figure out a way this guy could've vanished. I found no way possible. I know my father saw someone that day. He wouldn't make up something so odd just to freak us out, and even if he did, my father was not that good of an actor. This was also one of the last clear memories Pop had during those five months. After he took the postcard from his friend in the straw hat, his memory became very fuzzy.

Excerpt from Interview with Joe Hunter Sr.

Joe Sr.: *I had a hell of a time getting to sleep that night. After the whole thing with the old man at the door, I was leery. June and the kids tried to put my mind at ease telling me not to worry about it, but still talking to that man left me with a feeling of dread. I'll never forget the high pitch, singing tone of his voice when he said, "Hi".*

Pop woke up in the early morning hours the following day. From what he remembers, it was about two in the morning. This very prominent *thump* awoke him and he looked all over the bedroom, but could not identify its source. He got up and walked throughout the entire second and third floor. He checked on Mom and Marie. They were both sound asleep, but still the noise persisted.

Thump thump

Pop started down to the first floor, thinking maybe it was me or my brother James making the noise. If it was, there'd be hell to pay. Pop needed his sleep if he was going to drive his route in the morning. He slowly reached the landing and saw the light from the television glowing from the living room. His two boys were fast asleep. I was snoring like a monster, as I do. Unfortunately, I had inherited my mother's sinuses. After Pop checked on us he stepped into the kitchen and the 'heartbeat', as he would later call it when retelling this tale, seemed to get louder. The darkness didn't help the situation, but he didn't want to wake us up by turning on the kitchen light. He followed the heartbeat until he reached the window next to the stove, the window which had no business being there. My father stared out into the endless night and darkness until suddenly the heartbeat stopped. He would later claim every hair on his body had stood on end. He went to the fridge, got something to drink and went back to bed. How he got back to sleep is beyond me.

The next day he told everyone in the family what transpired and we tried to tell him he was asleep and that it was a dream. When in doubt, try the rational route first. He refused to believe it. He was sure it happened, and he was wide awake.

"I'm telling you, it happened. Why won't any of you believe me? Why would I make up something so stupid?" Pop was getting very irritated. In fact, ever since we moved into the new house, his temper was flaring a great deal more than it ever did previously.

"Pop, I'm sure it was just a dream," Mom said.

"Then why was my empty glass on the night table? Tell me that, damn it!"

"Maybe you were just sleep walking," Marie suggested.

My father never walked in his sleep before. In my lifetime, I've never seen him do that. The whole situation was odd.

"I don't think I was. I heard that heartbeat and followed it. I swear to God it was there," the fact we weren't buying his story upset the old man. In our defense, he had a history as a prankster. My family loved to play the game, who could scare the other person more. You had to be on your guard in the Hunter household.

After a few days, we put the postcard and the heartbeat behind us and focused on making the holler house a home. It wasn't easy. The worst were James and my rooms on the third floor. It was during our second or third week in the place I got the great idea to turn my bedroom into a poker room with a bar. It would not be easy, but I wanted to make my room into my place. My own personal haven. However, the house itself didn't like the idea. It made that very clear to me from day one.

The Poker Room and the Basement Bubble

Excerpt from interview with June and Joe Hunter Sr.:

June: *It concerned me what Virginia would say about us turning the room into a bar. We were only renting the place, but Joe wanted the kids to be comfortable.*

Joe Sr.: *I wasn't a fan of it because it meant he'd be sleeping on the couch all the time. Why have a bedroom and turn it into a poker room? But I wanted everyone to feel at home so I was ok with it if Virginia was ok with it.*

BACK IN 2006, TEXAS' hold' Em was huge. It was everywhere, and my friends and I got caught up in the craze. We played every chance we got. Mostly we played house games for very little money, but still it was a great time. Mike and I thought it would be a fantastic idea to make my bedroom, which I never would've slept in, into a bar/poker room where we could all hang out. I loved the idea.

Mom called up the landlady, and she said it was fine with her as long as it was all something we could take down if we moved. As soon as we got the ok, we began the project. Every one of my friends helped here and there, but most of the credit has to go to Dave and Mike. The two of them were over at the place every chance they got sanding and prepping the room for the work. We built a bar and bought the poker table and chairs. The floor around the bar had nice tile, and we even ran electric in the closet so we could put in a fridge and stereo system. Mike was the benefactor of this project. He provided a lot of the money which went into the poker room.

However, as the construction progressed, the environment in the house grew darker and colder, and I'm not talking about the winter temperatures. My father was irritable at every turn. He'd snap at anyone for any minor discretion. I remember him freaking out one day for the heat being turned up a bit.

"How hot do you people need it to be?" he bellowed as he readjusted the thermostat. It was freezing in the place, but oil was not cheap.

"Pop, it's cold in here," Marie pleaded.

"Put on a damn sweater! I'm sick of all the complaining about this house! You people don't like it, there's the door!" It was a horrible overreaction, and he slammed the basement door. It was his new routine. After he'd get home from work, he'd go check the bubble on the oil tank at least five times before going to bed. At first we thought he was just genuinely worried about running out of oil. Our family's first night in the house informed us just how cold it could get. The problem was, he'd be down there for an inordinate amount of time. Sometimes an entire hour and when we would inquire what he was doing down there, he'd snap at us.

"None of your damn business!" he screamed.

Pop always had a short fuse, but over the course of a few weeks in the house it was getting exponentially worse. The family walked on eggshells when around him, and we didn't dare give him any back talk. I became convinced he wasn't that far from becoming violent. This was a man who gave his family all he could, and now we lived in fear of him. It was so out of character for him. Mom was getting anxious about him.

Excerpt from Interview with Marie Hunter:

HOLLER HOUSE

Marie: *He was there. It was Mike. There is no question in my mind.*

ONE DAY WHILE I WAS at work, Mike was planning on coming over by himself to work on the poker room. I told Marie since she was going to be home to open the door and let him in. She was happy because it meant she wouldn't be alone in the house. It really didn't take long before we felt like we weren't alone. It appeared there were always eyes on you and you could quick look over your shoulder and catch someone or something staring back at you.

Marie was watching TV when there was knocking at the door. She opened it and there was Mike holding supplies for the day's job. He was going to start the arduous task of sanding the walls.

"Hey hun, did Joe tell you I was coming over today?" Mike asked.

"Yeah, come on in and head on up," she let him in and held the door for him.

Mike kissed her cheek and proceeded up to the third floor. For two hours she heard him banging and working up there as she watched daytime television. She was right in the middle of another show when another knock came at the door. This one surprised her because I told her Mike would be the only one coming over today. She just figured Dave or one of the other guys came to give Mike a hand, but when she opened the door she was in for a shock.

Standing before her was my old friend Mike. He smiled that same big grin at her and waited for her to open the door. His smile faded when he noticed the expression of bewilderment on her. He nearly dropped the supplies he was struggling to hold.

"Hey, didn't Joe tell you I was coming today to work on the poker room?" Mike broke the silence.

"How did you get down here without me seeing you?" Marie found her voice.

"What are you talking about?"

"Mike, you've been upstairs for the past two hours. I let you in myself!"

Mike stared at her in confusion. Marie told me he looked at her like she was a raving lunatic. He was speechless and didn't know what to say to her.

"Um Marie, this is the first time I've been here today. Can I come in and get to work, please?"

She nodded, and he briskly walked past her. She watched him ascend the stairs for the second time that day, and one nagging question remained with her. If Mike hadn't shown up yet, who was in the house with her for the last two hours?

When I got home from work and before I could get upstairs to help Mike, Marie told me about what happened. I had no answer for her. What was I going to say to her? She was losing her mind? Her boyfriend came and picked her up, and I tried to put the situation out of my mind and focus on the poker room. It was really the only joy I found in those five months of living there.

As time went on I, along with my brother, didn't like to be upstairs on the third floor alone. We just didn't feel safe. Both of us took to sleeping downstairs in the living room on the two sofas. I eventually asked James why he slept down with me and not up in his room. He asked me the same question.

"My room is a poker room. There's no bed in there. Where the hell would I sleep?"

He looked at me and rolled his eyes.

"That's a great excuse, Joe, but I'm willing to bet it is something else. I don't enjoy being up there by myself. I sleep down here with you because I feel safe. Sleeping in the same room with you is all I know."

This was a fully grown man who was also a bodybuilder, and he's scared to be in his own room alone. I knew he was right to be. He was also right about me using the poker room as an excuse. I already had trouble sleeping downstairs in the living room, let alone on the third floor. All of our fears and worries would become well founded over the following weeks.

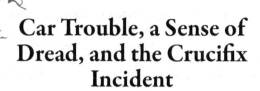

Car Trouble, a Sense of Dread, and the Crucifix Incident

Excerpt from interview with Joe Hunter Sr. and Marie Hunter

Joe Sr.: *Every morning I loved going to work. I'd wake up Marie or Mom and they'd go with me on my route. I realize now the primary reason I loved going to work was because I got to leave that awful place. Once I was out of there and many miles from the house I would feel great, like it lifted a weight off my chest.*

Marie: *When we were on the road, it was a blast. Dad was himself again. There was no undue anger and we would laugh and joke. As soon as we'd be heading home though, something ate at him. We would get about twenty minutes from the house and he'd start picking a fight for no reason. By the time we got to our front door, he'd be screaming at me or Mom over something. It was terrifying.*

EVERY FAMILY HAS THEIR fair share of car trouble and family spats with one another, but during this time period we filled our quota. In the short period we lived in the Holler House, the repairs and issues we endured with our vehicles were unheard of. Every week my family had to get a mechanic to see what was wrong with our cars. Also, during this time we were having trouble with our auto insurance. I firmly believe if Satan has a domain on Earth, it is the insurance industry.

My car and my brother's car got suspended for three months by our illustrious state capital, which meant the five of us depended on my father's car. This car was already getting a workout because of Pop's courier service. Only having one mode of transportation added to an already stressful situation.

The most prevalent problem with Pop's automobile was the tires. Damn near every week we had to shell out money for yet another tire. It made absolutely no sense. As soon as we'd replace one another would blow out. On multiple occasions, one of my friends and I needed to help Pop out while he was on his route. I really didn't mind going to help him out on the road. When Pop was out on the road, he was the same old Pop, laughing and joking with us, and not a care in the world. It really was the only time I could stand to be around him. In the time we lived in that damn house, our family set a record for blowing tires. Almost as if someone or something never wanted us to leave.

Over a brief period, I became increasingly distant and spent as little time as possible at home. If I was unfortunate enough to be at home on any given day and Pop was there, he subjected me to a string of vile verbal assaults. Most of them revolved around me never being able to do anything right. My friends and I were continuing to renovate my poker room and the further we got to completing the project, the angrier Pop got.

"You should've kept it a damn bedroom," he shouted at me during one day, while I was sanding the walls. "Look at what you've done to this place. Why didn't you just stay in college? You obviously can't make a living with your hands."

I desperately tried to ignore him, but he eventually provoked a screaming match and I'd storm out, call one of my friends and be out till the early morning hours. I tried to not return until I was sure he'd be asleep. This was a man I shared a fantastic relationship with throughout my life, and now I found I had nothing but contempt and hatred for him.

I recall a day I was home with my sister Marie. Mom had the day off and she rode with Pop. He enjoyed having some company on the road, usually it was Marie. We were in the living room watching a movie and I could tell she wanted to ask me something, but she wasn't sure how to broach the subject.

"Have you been noticing the difference in Pop?" she finally broke the silence.

"You'd have to be a blind man not to. He has become a colossal prick. I'm not sure why he hates me so much," I responded and surprised myself because I felt tears coming.

"He doesn't hate you, Joey. He was just saying the other day when we were out, 'I can't understand why Joe is never home?' He really misses you. When you aren't working you are out with your friends or spending the night somewhere else."

I paused the movie.

"Why the hell would I want to be here when he is here? All he does is criticize me or berate me for not staying in school or having a better job. He is on my back constantly."

"I know and I asked him why he acts like that; what he said makes me anxious."

Marie took a deep breath, and I watched tears bobble down her cheeks. "He has no memory of ever fighting with you when you two are home. All he knows is you aren't around anymore and he can't understand why. Joey, how can that be? Is he sick? Maybe he's having blackouts?"

It seemed very farfetched, or maybe a copout. Behaving so poorly toward your family and then claiming sudden amnesia. I really didn't believe it, but at this point I didn't really care what his excuse was. Our relationship had become so strained by that point, all I wanted was to be away from him. Some days I wished he wouldn't come home at all. What a horrible thought for a son to have.

"I don't know what his problem is Lil Sis," I said, "All I know is he shows me nothing but hate when he and I are home."

"He's not like that on the road Joey," Marie wiped the moisture from her eyes. "We have a lot of fun when we're out. I asked him last week why he gets so mad when we head back home? 'I can feel this heaviness in my chest. The closer we get to the house, the heavier it gets. It's like a feeling of dread I can't explain. Marie I hate that place; I think I made a mistake moving us in there, but we're stuck now.'"

Pop wasn't wrong, we didn't have the financial means to move. I overheard a few conversations between my parents about not being able to make the rent because of all the auto problems. Also, oil prices were continuing to rise.

"He's not making that part up Joey; don't tell me you don't feel that same feeling of dread when you're in this place. I'm constantly being watched by someone and I can't explain it."

"It's an old house, Marie, and we've only been here a few months. We have to get used to it. Don't worry, I'm sure things will get better. Pop is just stressed out about the new place." I knew I was giving her a line of bullshit, but I was trying to calm her down. The place scared Marie and as the big brother it was my job to protect her. How could I protect her from something none of us could explain? I hugged her, and we finished watching the movie, trying our best to put our troubles out of our mind. Yet we knew in a few hours a man would walk through that door and he wasn't the loving father we knew. Pop was becoming something so much worse, and evidently he did not understand it was happening.

Excerpt from Interview with Joe Hunter Sr.

Joe Sr.: *My mother raised me a strict Catholic and I have never laid a hand on my wife, or any other woman. I have no memory of this happening, but I have no reason to believe June or Marie would make up such a story.*

HOLLER HOUSE

I WAS AT WORK WHEN Marie called me in hysterics. She was crying and the only words I could decipher were, *he's gonna hurt Mom.* I told her to have Zack come pick me up because I still didn't have a damn car. My boss didn't give me any problems for leaving early because she saw my expression. Zack and Marie got there in record time and I jumped in the car. The story they told me made me want to kill Pop. I've never been so angry in my life.

"Joey, I've never seen him like that before," Marie cried. Her face was beet red from crying and her voice was hoarse. "He just came at Mom!"

"Calm down and tell me what happened," I tried my best to keep my cool.

Marie began, but her voice broke and another wave of tears came. Her boyfriend Zack had to relay what happened that morning. Zack associated with my family for several years and he was a good guy. He treated my sister very well, but that day he was so unnerved.

"Pop was upstairs getting ready for his route and we found out he blew another tire, he told Mom he needed money to get a new one. She told him he'd have to wait for her to get paid at the end of the week and Pop went ape shit!"

A hard sob from Marie interrupted him.

"He was at the second floor landing and the next thing we know he grabs your grandfather's crucifix off the wall and throws it down the stairs at Mom."

"Did it hit her?" I asked, my rage growing with every word he said.

"No, but then he came running down the steps and grabs the cross, pushes Mom against the wall, and holds the cross to her throat."

Marie bellowed, "Joey he told her if she moved he'd slit her throat and when I screamed at him to stop, he called me a bitch and told me to 'shut up', but Joey it wasn't Pop!"

"What do you mean?" her words left me confused. If it wasn't the old man than who was it?

"His voice became distorted and when he turned to face me, he had a disfigured face! I hit his wrist with a mug and he dropped the cross."

"Zack, where the hell were you when he had a hold of my mother?"

"Joe, what was I supposed to do? It's Pop for Christ's sake," Zack was defending himself and he had a point. He held my father in a very high regard. The thought of laying a hand on him was unthinkable.

"He dropped the cross, and it was like he woke up. He hugged mom and apologized to her and me. Joey, I don't understand what's going on!"

We got back to the house and Pop and Mom were in the kitchen trying to figure out how to get the tire fixed yet again. I walked in ready for war. My father and I never came to blows, but this was as close as we would ever get.

"What the hell is going on?" I came in yelling.

"You better remember who you're talking to boy," Pop got right in my face and Mom jumped up from the table to get between us.

"I get a call from work telling me you're attacking Mom? What the hell is wrong with you? Mom, are you alright?"

Mom nodded and pleaded with her eyes for me not to escalate the situation.

"She's fine, and this is none of your business. I'll bet your lazy ass couldn't wait to get out of work again."

I wanted to take his head off. Even in this scenario where he was in the wrong, he had the balls to talk down to me. It wasn't my father. Of that I was certain at that point. Zack and Marie got the tire fixed, and the family tried to put the ugly mess behind us, but something changed that day in my mother.

Later that night Mom and Marie were at the local Laundromat because the house didn't have a dryer. Later I found out the conversation which transpired between them. Marie informed me the two of them were discussing the best method for killing Pop. How they could end it quietly and where they could dispose of the body. The situation got so bad so quickly in that house, my mother and sister were desperate enough to commit murder. Fear and hate are powerful motivators, and the man who was living in that house with us was scaring the hell out of his family.

Excerpt from interview with Marie Hunter:

Marie: *He was asleep but awake. I did not understand what he was doing in my bedroom.*

IT WAS TWO THIRTY IN the morning and the banging over her bed had awoken Marie. She saw the man who raised her and loved her standing there banging on the closet door, whispering to himself, "Open it, open it!"

"Pop, I can't open it, my bed is in the way," she tried to explain to him and keep her cool, but terror consumed her.

"I'll open the damn thing," Pop slowly turned his head and glared at her. She later told me his eyes were open, but he wasn't there. He stomped back to his room and went back to sleep. Marie went down to the kitchen and grabbed a butcher's knife. From then on, that knife was under my sister's pillow.

The next morning, she told my mother and me about the previous night. Pop was up in the shower and once again we heard him cursing it. The shower was odd in its own right. Every time one of us went to use the damn thing, it never worked properly. The water would freeze one minute and slowly become just warm enough to shower. Then it would become scolding hot and several times it even burned us. My father seemed to be the prime target of the shower's aggression. More than once we'd hear him scream from the bathroom, "Oh God, it burned my balls!"

He'd come barreling out from upstairs with a towel around him, scream at us for doing something to the water. None of us ever did. Maybe it was just a bad water heater or something wrong with the pipes, but it only added to a dangerous situation. After hearing what Marie had to share about the closet and the butcher knife, Mom and I were finally ready to do something about this.

"Marie, go find that damn postcard and take it up to Virginia's house. It's time we got some answers about what the hell is going on in this place. I want the man I married back and that old woman must know something."

Pieces of the Past Revealed and the Three Stages

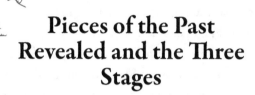

Excerpt from interview with Marie Hunter:
Marie: *There were hundreds of them, the same one repeatedly.*

AFTER HEARING WHAT my sister found out when she visited the old woman, it was no wander she could afford to rent the place out for such a cheap rate. Virginia was incredibly well off and her house was proof of it. Her family practically built Pebble creek and the community surrounding it. She'd mentioned when we met, her family had gained the land in 1860, which meant they were people of means, but Marie did not understand how wealthy they were.

Virginia's home was like a museum completely laden with antique furniture and bobbles which were showing their age and value. Virginia did not hide her finer things either. For God's sake, her house literally sat on a hill overlooking the common folk. She served my sister a cup of tea with a sterling silver tea set. It was all very decadent and the exact opposite of what the Hunters were used to.

"Have you come to drop off the rent, my dear?" Virginia's hand shook as she poured Marie a cup of steaming hot tea.

"Yes, and I have something for you from our house," Marie pulled the postcard out of her jacket pocket.

Virginia reached for her glasses almost irritably; maybe she hated showing her age to one so young. When she held the picture up to her nose, she laid it down on her lap and gave my sister a knowing glance.

"I figured this would happen again," the old woman let out a heavy sigh. "Every damn time I get a new tenant."

"You knew about this picture?" Marie sipped at her hot tea.

"Oh, I knew dear. Look at the shoe box on the shelf over there and bring it here. At my age, it's easier if you do it. If I do it, we'd be here all night and I'm sure you've got places to be."

Marie made her way over to the shelf and reached up for the yellowed box. For just being a shoe box, it had some serious heft to it. She brought it over to Virginia and placed it in her lap. Virginia carefully opened up the aged box and Marie was no longer surprised by the weight of it. Inside filled to the brim was the same postcard, the same picture as the one the man handed Pop.

"Dear, I have so many of these. Most are from people around Pebble Creek. They know my family still owns the land, and they think it's nice to give it to me. A reminder of days gone. I always take it and tell them thank you and act like I've never seen it before, just to be polite. However, the ones I get from my tenants are always the most surprising."

"Why is that Virginia?" the tale enthralled Marie.

"Well, the ones I get from them always have writing on the back. It's always an unfamiliar name, but the message is usually the same thing. Most of the time it's, 'Having a good time and learning a lot, Sloan is taking care of us.'"

"Sloan, who's Sloan?" Marie asked.

Virginia's expression told Marie she wished she never mention his name. Her sweet elderly visage suddenly became very troubled and put out. The old woman lightly tapped the box in her lap and stared past Marie. Marie later told me it seemed like she was looking into the past to get the story just right.

"Back when the old house was still a mill, many children would go there during the summer for extra work and do odd jobs here and there. Their parents never worried because they loved that their kids were showing some work ethic, which is something a lot of today's youth can't do. No offense, dear."

Marie shook her head and waved her hand.

"The caretaker or foreman of the mill was a short man by the name of Sloan. He supervised the daily routine at the mill and kept watch over the little ones while they were there."

"Did your family know him?"

"Oh yes, if fact he was family, a distant cousin or something like that. Well, it got out to the community Sloan enjoyed the company of the little ones a bit too much, if you know what I mean?"

Marie nodded, but the thought made her skin crawl.

"Apparently he would make the children write these postcards to their parents to show they were in no danger. When word got out about what the creep was doing, he disappeared one night. They never saw him again."

Virginian dug through the shoebox until she found what she was looking for. Marie's eyes widened as she saw a picture of the man our father described perfectly, the same overalls and the same straw hat, and no shoes.

"No shoes," Marie whispered to herself.

"That's right dear; he was famous for that before being a kiddy diddler. The man never wore shoes."

"Virginia, this man came to our house and gave that picture to my father."

"No Marie," dismissed Virginia, "They all say that, but that is not possible, not at all. They discovered Sloan's body a few counties over after he vanished. He was face down in a ditch. Too good for him if you ask me. That was back in the 1800s before my family even owned the property."

The chill in Marie's spine slowly made its way down and every hair on her body was standing on end. Pop hadn't lied to them, and there was absolutely no way he could have known this.

"I have to go, Virginia. Thank you for the tea," Marie quickly got out of her chair and grabbed her keys.

"Do you want this back, after all it's yours," Virginia handed the post card back to her.

Marie raised her hands in refusal. There was no way she wanted to touch that picture again, knowing full well where it came from.

"No, I believe you should have it, after all it *really* belongs to you."

"How do you mean, dear?"

"I'm not sure when, but you filled out that post card. That's your name on the back of that picture." Marie walked out of the room.

The old woman, quicker than she'd done anything before I'd wager, spun it around in horror to make sure if Marie was telling her the truth.

My sister was no liar.

Excerpt from interview with Joe Hunter Sr.:

Joe Sr.: *It was like this heaviness constantly bearing down on me. I could feel it in my chest, making it difficult to breathe.*

I SPENT AS MUCH OF my time away from that damn house as I could. After we finished the poker room, and the guys and I played a few games there, the fun stopped. My father was constantly riding me about this or that. Nothing I did was right, and everything I did was wrong in his eyes. So avoiding yet another argument I'd go to work, hang out with my friends as much as possible, or spend some time with my other group of friends at the local college.

While I never attended a single class at the school, I knew plenty of people there. I partied there and I really wish I remembered more. I remember the people closest to me, however. One of them was Milly and while she may have had her quirks, she was a good person. I confided in her one drunken night about the situation at the holler house.

Her eyes shined with intrigue as I relayed the history of the place and the transformation my father was going through. Milly possessed a fascination with the paranormal and the occult in all its incarnations. They lined her book shelf with one book after another, dealing with some form of supernatural. Milly herself even looked the part. The persona she tried desperately to project to the world was your typical pale, gothic teen with plenty of piercings to match. Inside Milly was a very lonely girl though, and her stories, sometimes they were outlandish, were very entertaining. She was a superb listener when I needed to vent.

"I'm just not sure what the hell to do anymore," I took another swig of Smirnoff Ice as I regaled her with yet another woeful tale of my father and mine's deteriorating relationship. Yes, I was one of those misinformed youths who drank Smirnoff Ice. Back in those days, I could not stand the taste of beer. Thank God my taste buds changed as I got older.

"I've met your dad Joe, he seemed cool to me," she replied.

"It's like he's a different person since we moved into that damn place. Also, Marie told me when he's out on the road he is the same old Pop we used to know. Only when they're on their way home does he feel it."

Milly stopped the bottle before it hit her lips. My story finally piqued her interest.

"Feel what?" she asked.

"I'm not sure how to describe it. Marie said, 'he feels like this pressure on his chest that radiates throughout his entire body and by the time he gets home he's in such a foul mood.' Every night he's picking a fight with one of us over the littlest thing."

I did not notice until I felt it drop off my face; I was crying. It was all so emotionally taxing. Pop and I were so close and to watch him grow into someone who hated me, and someone who I hated in return, was almost unbearable. My friends were my only salvation during those horrible months.

"Joe, what your dad is describing sounds like oppression," Milly set her bottle down and retrieved one of her thicker books off the shelf. "Oppression is one of the three stages of possession. It's the second stage to be more accurate."

"You think something possessed my dad, Mills," I scoffed and wiped my eyes, "Maybe he's just an asshole."

"I don't want to worry you, but it sure sounds like it. See, the three stages are infestation, oppression and finally possession. You really don't want to get to the third stage cause that's where you vomit pea soup and they make an awful movie about it."

I laughed. It felt good to laugh.

"The first stage is infestation, and that's when you hear the bumps in the night, or the feeling of eyes on you which you've mentioned about the place."

My mind instantly flashed to the story Pop told all of us about the heartbeat.

"Oppression is basically where the presence, demon, or entity completely obliterates the person who it finds to be the most vulnerable."

"Milly there are many ways one could describe my father but none of them would be 'vulnerable,'" I disagreed.

"He puts up a good front, Joe, but put yourself in his shoes for a second. He moves his family from the only home they've ever known and into this ancient house, which needs a lot of work, all the while trying to run his own business. Wouldn't the stress be incredible for anyone? All that stress leaves a person susceptible to certain things."

She made an excellent point. I was in my early twenties and barely had any responsibilities. I never stopped to consider my father's worries. In finally doing so, sympathy replaced a bit of the rage I was harboring.

"If Pop is in the middle of stage 2, as you say, what do we do to pull him out of it?"

"Well, the books I've read say you need to know who or what you're dealing with. You need to identify what the hell it is before you can know how to fight it. Other than that pervert Sloan and his damn postcards, do you have any idea what else it could be?"

I downed the rest of my drink in one long gulp and shook my head.

"It's an old house, Joe. Two hundred years of history have passed through those walls. You need to figure out what it is, and sooner rather than later. It's only been a few months and your dad is already in stage two. This thing works fast."

Her words sent quivers down my spine. I wasn't aware of it then, but a massive puzzle piece was about to fall into my lap. It would come in the form of a dream and a warning. One I could not ignore for fear it would mean my family's destruction.

BAD DREAMS AND
ONE GOOD MEMORY

Excerpt from Interview with Marie Hunter:
　　Marie: *Joey told me about his dream and I just wasn't sure if we could trust it. I mean, who the hell was Lenny and was he on the level?*

I BELIEVE EVERY ONE of us on planet Earth contains within us some form of psychic ability. Whether you are a full fledge medium and can communicate with the dead one on one, or your empathy is so great you can legitimately feel the energy in a room and take on said energy. I feel very sorry for empaths because most of the time the feelings they receive are sorrow and pain, the most palpable of human emotions.

Whatever your belief is about the supernatural, it usually takes one unexplainable event to turn a skeptic into a believer. While I hold firm to my beliefs on the matter, I first and foremost apply a healthy dose of skepticism when dealing with anything paranormal. One should always look for a rational explanation before jumping to other worldly conclusions. After we have exhausted all earthly avenues, then it's time to look at possible paranormal theories. What happened a few nights after my conversation with Milly gave me *actual cause* to believe something otherworldly was going on.

I've described this to my wife and a few close friends in the past, and somewhere along the retelling they usually give me a subtle eye roll or a patronizing nod. Whether it was just a very vivid dream or a warning from the *great beyond* I will never know for sure, but what it for sure is, the information it gave me in the dream was accurate.

My brother and I were sleeping down on in the living room, which became our pseudo bedroom. If we went upstairs in James' room at all, it was to get dressed and that was it. My poker room was across the very narrow hallway and over time I began to not even feel safe in that room, but I never felt safe in my brother's room. We were both sleeping soundly, when suddenly my eyes opened and it felt like we were not alone in the living room anymore. I sat up and sitting in my father's recliner was this middle age man dressed in a plaid shirt, black pants, and a brown fedora. He resembled an extra in an old gangster flick. I half expected Joe Pesci to come in the house and *whack* the guy right in front of me. I was very nervous and scared to death. At first I thought we had a break in, but then I noticed his pale complexion and the sadness in his eyes.

This man was dead... and smiling.

"Relax kid, I'm not here to hurt you or him," he gestured toward James who was fast asleep.

"Who are you and why are you in our house?" I asked, trying not to let my voice break.

"The name's Lenard but most of my friends call me Lenny, and I think it's cute you believe this is your house."

Goosebumps covered every inch of my body. His words although not meant to threaten me carried a sense of foreboding. I pulled my blanket closer to my chest. Isn't it fascinating even as adults we reach for our blankets when fear presents itself?

"Do you have any idea what's going on in this place? Since the moment you guys moved into the joint, you've been in danger," Lenny explained.

"How do you know that?"

"I've been here awhile, kid, since back when this place was hopping. This place used to be one hell of juke joint and a place where a regular Joe, such as me, could enjoy a lady of the evening."

"It was a forge and a mill," I corrected him.

The corners of Lenny's mouth curved upward into a wide grin. As we talked, I felt more comfortable with him. I never got a threat of danger from him.

"Boy, should I let you tell the story? This was back in the 1940s son, your Ma and Pop weren't even an idea yet."

"Why didn't Virginia mention..."

"She don't know it kid, this was all done on the sly," he interrupted me.

Even if the old woman knew about it, I doubt she would've told us. It's not exactly a selling point when trying to rent out a family home. Still, there was a possibility she didn't know it.

"You died here, didn't you?" it was abrupt, but I said it anyway.

"Oh yeah, I did, got my damn neck broken on those stupid narrow steps in the basement. It was so stupid of me and I never saw it coming, but hey at least it was quick right?" he pulled the collar of his shirt open and I saw the disjointed neck bone. It made me shiver.

"Were you pushed or was it an accident?"

"Does it really matter, kid? It all means one thing... I'm dead."

"My dad's down in the basement a lot lately. I hate it down there and he should too. Too many spider webs and it's so dark down there. He tells us he's checking the bubble, but he'll be down there for an hour some nights. We don't know what he's doing."

"I'd like to say it's all going to work out for you guys, but it won't if you keep living here. Things are going to get worse for your old man and the rest of you. This place is not for the living boy. Too much history and too much nasty stuff. The land just soaks it up and makes it its own. You need to get the hell out of this house."

James' let out a loud snore and rolled over on his side. I was glad he was asleep for this conversation.

"I don't know how to get us out of here. Mom and Pop don't have any money, and our lease has us stuck here. Why can't you and the other ghost here just leave my family alone?"

Lenny became downtrodden. His brow furrowed with sorrow.

"It's not us kid... it's *her.*"

Without warning there was an enormous bang from the second floor landing as if someone dropped a damn anvil. I immediately sat up and was wide awake. My eyes shot to the recliner, and it was empty but still slightly rocking back and forth. James sat up and wiped the sleep from his eyes.

"What was that, Joe?" James was groggy but alert.

"Nothing bro, go back to sleep," I didn't want to scare him any further. I was already trembling enough for the both of us. That was the first and the last time I ever saw Lenny and to this day I'm really not sure if he was real or not, but his final word cut me to the core. Who did he mean when he said, "her"?

Excerpt from interview with June Hunter:

June: *It was fantastic; we were a family again if only for an evening.*

ONE OF THE FEW PLEASANT experiences we had in the house was on a snowy Saturday evening in February. I remember no one could leave the house because of the snow, and I wasn't happy because I hated being home, especially on a Saturday night. However, Mother Nature had other plans, and they involved eight inches of fresh snow. Maybe it was God's way of telling us to cling tight to each other. The few holidays we spent in the place were not memorable. For Christmas, no one could afford presents and we didn't even have a tree. So we all sat around drinking cherry whiskey, which was tasty till we fell asleep watching TV. That night however went from being a disappointment to being a reminder we were a family.

Mom made us all toasted cheese sandwiches and tomato soup, I always referred to it as "poor man's feast", and on a cold winter night it hit the spot. After that, we sat at the kitchen table playing cards. We were all laughing and joking, even Pop. During the fun, he got up to check the basement bubble again. I really didn't want him to go down in the basement.

"No Pop sit down I'll go check on it," I offered.

He seemed surprised, but he didn't argue, "there's a good boy, just tell me where it's at and please don't touch my desk down there. I've got it just the way I want it."

I reached for the doorknob to the basement and paused. The few times I'd been down there, I'd seen no desk, and neither had anyone else. I got down there and immediately felt the eyes on me. Whatever it was, was here. I quickly checked the oil tank and turned and noticed the area behind the steps where an old shelf was. There were footprints there. I examined the prints; they looked like Pop's work boots, but the disturbing thing was a matted down area in the dirt floor. It looked like someone had been sitting there and again, there was no desk to speak of in the basement.

"Hey Joey let's go, you're holding the game up!" Marie yelled down the steps. Her voice jarred me from my own thoughts and I was glad for it. The revelation that I was staring at my father's 'desk' scared the hell out of me.

I came back up the stairs and acted like nothing was wrong. I couldn't spoil the fun we had that night. It was so long since we were all happy together, so long since we heard my father laugh and joke with us at home. I know it's a cliché, but you really don't truly miss something until it's gone. This was the last time we were the Hunters until we moved out of that God forsaken hell hole.

Miss Mary Mack... All Dressed in Black

Excerpt from interview with Marie Hunter:

Marie: *I called Joey frantic; there was no way I was going to stay in that house all alone!*

MY MOTHER WAS THE FIRST to see her. Evidently the incident occurred two weeks after we moved into the place. Mom wasn't one hundred percent sure she had seen it to begin with, but either way she didn't want to worry us or scare us. She left that to whatever the hell was in the Holler House.

Mom was the first one up that morning. She was getting ready to work her early shift and making Pop's coffee as she always did. With the coffee brewing, she set about getting herself ready. It was during this process she incidentally passed through the small entryway between the living room and the kitchen and caught something out of the corner of her eye. Isn't that always the way? I've often wondered why most spirits or entities live in our periphery.

Mom glanced up the steps to the second floor landing and stood frozen in fear. Standing there was a woman. From the way she tells it, "It was unmistakably a female and from the look she was giving me, she wanted no part of us being in *her* house."

A lifetime passed as the two women stared at each other. My mother's heart beat so fast she was sure she wouldn't need her coffee for the next several months. The woman on the stairs wore an old-fashioned dress with frilly lace around the collar and at the ends of her sleeves. Her hair up in a bun. Although the interaction only lasted a few moments, the image seared itself into my Mother's memory forever.

Excerpt from interview with June Hunter:

June: *She stared at me with that dreadful scowl, and I instantly felt threatened. My mind was racing as we locked eyes and all I could do was stand there. The next thing I knew, she moved into Marie's room. I hesitate to say she walked. It was as if she floated. My protective instincts kicked in then, and I tore up those steps. I rounded the corner and there was Marie, sleeping soundly. When I turned around, I got another shock. Pop was standing behind me and scared me to death. It irritated him as my stomping up the steps woke him up.*

A FEW WEEKS PASSED and Mom tried and put the whole unpleasant business out of her mind. However, try as she could, the woman in black was there in her mind and around every corner in the house.

The next interaction with *her* was my Father's, but he was more vocal about the event. He'd been in the middle of a heavy sleep when his eyes shot open for no rational reason. He sat right up and looked around his dark bedroom. The moonlight was pouring in through the windows, offering little illumination.

Excerpt from interview with Joe Hunter Sr:

Joe: *I just had this overwhelming urge to go up to the third floor and check it out. It was annoying because it was so late and I was so tired. I hated getting up at night in that damn place. The floor was always freezing and the creep factor was undeniable, but that night I couldn't shake the feeling of going to the third floor. So up I went, opening the door to the third floor, trying to be silent so as not to wake anybody up. The light was on in Joe's poker room, which bugged the hell out of me. I constantly told him to turn the damn thing out. I was half tempted to go down and drag his ass up there to turn it off. I went up to turn the light off and checked James' bedroom. I flicked off the light switch and turned to walk through the beaded curtain heading back down the steps... and there she was. I stopped on a dime. We were face to face, inches apart. If I could have moved my arms, I could have clocked her in the head. She just glared at me with those horrible eyes. Every hair on my body was on end and I froze. I finally closed my eyes and when I opened them again, she was at the bottom of the steps looking up at me. I watched her enter my bedroom and raced down the steps, fearing she was going after June.*

THE NEXT MORNING POP woke up and told Mom and Marie. Again Marie played it off as if Pop was just dreaming. Mom knew he was telling the truth, but still to spare Marie from the terror she and my Father were now enduring, she agreed he was dreaming. In retrospect, she wished she would have told Pop everything at that point. It might have expedited us moving out and getting somewhere safe.

That no one believed him was infuriating. It's hard for me to blame the house or any other exterior forces on his anger that day. He cussed out the two of them and refused to talk to them for the rest of the day. He spent the rest of the day in his bedroom, only coming out to check the oil in the basement. The next day when he and Marie were out on his route, he didn't even bring it up. He was laughing and joking with her the entire day until they headed back home. Within fifteen minutes of the house, he went quiet again.

Over the first month or two, I made it a point to stay away whenever I could. I was developing a profound hatred for my Father. It just seemed to me and my family I had a target on my back for his aggression. All I'd have to say is good morning or something as innocent as that, and he'd freak out on me. During one particularly awful rant, he informed me how much of a disappointment I was because I didn't stay in college. He screamed I'd never amount to anything. When Mom and Marie tried to intervene, he shut them down with an ugly look. So I stayed away.

The local diner became my sanctuary. No matter what the boys and I were doing, the night would always end with a bullshit session at the diner. It was really the only time I found any happiness; my friends knew nothing of what was going on in the house. All they knew was Pop, and I were at odds constantly.

One night the guys got a taste of what was going on. We were at the diner around nine at night and my cell phone went off. I almost ignored the call, but it was from Marie. Thank God I didn't ignore the call.

"Hey Lil Sis, what's up?"

"Joey, you've got to come get me! Zack couldn't come and Duke…" Marie was in hysterics. She was sobbing so hard I barely made out what she was saying. The last part I got from her before the phone cut out was, "She's… here!"

Mike and I jumped into his car and raced back to the house to get her. It scared me to think someone had broken into the house and attacked my sister. Poor Mike had me yelling in his ear for the brief trip back to the house, telling him to speed up. When we pulled into the drive Marie was pacing around out front. She wouldn't even go near the front porch and had turned every light in the joint on. Mike and I got out, and she buried her head in my chest with deep, hysterical sobs. I tried to calm her down, but she just kept crying. It was almost too much to bear.

Excerpt from interview with Marie Hunter:

Marie: *Mom and Pop had left about an hour before I called Joey. A few weeks prior Pop got an alternative route and could make extra money doing it at night. He loved it because it was more time spent away from the house. Mom and I usually went with him, but on that night I was very ill and stayed home with my boyfriend Zack. However, Zack couldn't come over that night because his Mom grounded him. So it was just me and the dogs. I was in the living room watching TV when I heard Duke, our beagle, start whimpering in the kitchen. I got up to go check on him and I saw him below the window barking at it. He wouldn't leave that window alone. So I grabbed him by the collar and pulled him into the living room. He wasn't an enormous dog, but I had a hell of a time dragging him out of the kitchen. He never took his eyes off the window until we got to the landing of the steps. Duke began barking and howling toward the second floor and I looked up there and there she was, in all her glory. She was exactly how Pop described, and later Mom would confirm she saw her too. The expression she had was so threatening and frightening for a moment, I couldn't move. I started screaming at her 'who are you, what do you want? You don't belong here!' She just kept staring at me until I ran out of the house and called Joey. The reception in the house was awful, and you needed to go outside for a signal, which was no problem that night because*

I wanted no part of that house. He picked up, and the phone crackled and cut out. And I couldn't get him back. So there I stood in the cold, sick, scared out of my wits, and all alone. It seemed like an eternity till Mike and Joey pulled up, but when they did, I ran and have never held my big brother tighter.

AFTER MIKE AND I WENT through the house and checked to make sure someone wasn't in there, we made sure we turned the lights off. The three of us got back to the diner and on the way Marie explained what occurred in the house. Although I was a believer, I still had not seen this woman for myself and whether I felt Marie was telling me the truth or not, the terror she felt was undeniable. She'd definitely seen someone or something on those stairs. We all stayed up at the diner and I finally got her calmed down, but then my cell went off again. This time it was my Father screaming at me through the phone.

"Where the hell are you and your sister? The dogs are here by themselves and every light in the damn house is on!" Pop's words were so loud Mike heard them. Both of us stared at each other, knowing we shut every single light off in the place.

"We're up at the diner. Marie called me freaking out, she said there was someone in the house so we came and picked her up," I tried to explain but any explanation from me to my Father at this point in our relationship was unacceptable. He continued to berate me until he finally hung up on me. I wanted so badly to whip the phone across the restaurant, but I couldn't afford a new phone.

"Joey, she was there, I saw her, and she *was* there!" Marie was on the verge of tears again.

"I believe you Marie, I just wish there was something we could do about it."

"We have to go back, don't we?" she asked. Her hands were shaking now.

I nodded and took her trembling hand in mine.

"Joey, I can't be alone in that house again... I *won't* be alone in that house again."

The poker room seemed like somewhat of a haven for me in the house, though not much of one. I was hosting at least one game a week on the third floor of that house and the boys would come over and we'd have some fun. I stocked the mini fridge with whatever brand of soda I could afford. Usually, the generic store stuff. It surprised me Pop never objected to me having the games late at night. He said he didn't mind as long as we kept it down and we did. The last thing I wanted to do was wake him up.

I was setting up for yet another poker game one night, a few weeks after the incident with Marie. I was counting out the chip amounts and setting them in place, listening to my young, angry music and marveling at the job we'd done in the room. To this day I'm not sure why I went with blood red for the paint, but crimson surrounded me. Maybe it reflected how life was going for me?

I sat there shuffling the cards and waiting to hear the sounds of footsteps coming up the steps. I heard the door from the second floor open and close, but when I looked at my beaded curtain, it wasn't a friend who was staring back at me. At the diner that night, Marie described her by calling her Miss Mary Mack. I didn't get the reference until Marie recited the old children's rhyme.

"Miss Mary Mack, Mack, Mack, all dressed in black, black, black. With silver buttons, all down her back, back, back."

I sat there holding the deck of playing cards, staring at the evil visage of this vile woman. I swear I heard the haunting tones of my sister repeating the rhyme. My mind also flashed to the dream where Lenny warned me, "it wasn't him, it was... *her.*"

We locked eyes and neither one of us would blink. It wasn't out of bravery; it wasn't a brave moment for me. I didn't want to blink for fear she would get closer if I took my eyes off her. I struggled to find the courage to speak, but deep down I regain my powers of speech.

"I don't know who or what you are, but this is not your house anymore. You're not welcome here and I want you to leave my family alone. Stop tormenting my Father, he is a good man, and he loves us. Leave us alone," I was calm but assertive. My voice cracked a few times, but I figured I got my point across. Yet my efforts seemed in vain as my otherworldly opponent slowly and methodically shook her head from side to side. It was the only response I got from her, but it was more than enough.

A car pulled up and its lights caused me to look out the window and when I looked back old Mary Mack was not there, but I knew that night I'd come face to face with evil. It was the first and the last time I saw her, but her presence permeated throughout the house. I don't think she was the only entity in the place, but I'm very certain she was the dominant one. To add insult to injury, I lost money that night in the poker game.

In Sickness and in Hell

Excerpt from interview with June Hunter:

June: *I felt God awful while we lived in that place. I can't remember one week where someone in the house wasn't throwing up or coughing. Towards the end, I really believed one of us was going to die.*

THREE MONTHS IN AND our lives were getting progressively worse. Putting aside all the supernatural elements we were contending with, Mom, Marie, and I all began getting ill. At first we figured it was just the overall temperature in the place. We just could not get warm enough. I usually burn hot and am not a cold person, but while we lived there, I wore sweatshirts all the time.

Mom was the first one to get gravely sick. For several weeks, she couldn't keep any food down and was living off a very bland diet. It started as a headache, then chills, and finally attacked her stomach. Marie was showing signs of the same illness, and both of them needed several trips to the doctor before they hit the road to recovery. While the symptoms ended up subsiding, a few of them lingered till we left the place.

I was in asthmatic Hell living there. To make matters worse, I didn't have health insurance and was relying on my grandmother to get medication. My lungs were constantly fighting to breathe, and I was using breathing treatments several times a week just to make it to work. When I was away from home, it wasn't nearly as bad, but I'd still be hacking up a lung. It convinced Mom it was the house. Whatever evil was manipulating my Father was now coming after us directly.

My brother James wasn't at home enough to experience any of the effects of the house. Because of his job on third shift and trying to get his acting/model's career off the ground, he was never home. I was envious of him. Later on in life he confessed to me he was so frightened while inside the house, he would find any reason to stay away.

Like James, Pop too was not getting sick and he would lash out at those of us that were. It altered his behavior and personality by the day, but again it was only when he was at home. Marie and Mom often reminded me he was fine when he was on the road. He showed genuine concern for all of us while at work and grew more worried about our health. Yet as soon as he'd walk into his house, the switch would flip.

"You people are just too weak. No immune system to speak of," Pop proclaimed one night at dinner. Mom, Marie, and I just stared at our plates in silence. He slapped me on the shoulder and continued, "I can't believe my son can't get over a little cough."

My hatred and resentment for him was at its highest level. I wanted to take the fork in my hand and tear his throat out with it. He wasn't my father anymore. By then he'd become the source of all my woes. Mom and Marie still worried about him, but I wished he wouldn't wake up some mornings. I know it's a horrible thing to think, but we all were reaching our breaking point.

The house was winning.

Excerpt from Interview with Joe Hunter Sr:

Joe Sr.: *I hate wine. I've never been a wine drinker, but apparently I was making June pick up wine whenever she was out.*

WE SAT THERE EATING dinner, and I watched Pop drink three or four glasses of wine with his meal. This may not sound important unless you factor in that my Father, in all his life, had never been a wine drinker. He hated wine and on the rare occasion he had alcohol; it was beer or whiskey. It wasn't even excellent wine. It was that cheap boxed wine some hobos wouldn't even touch.

Pop was finishing his latest glass and going for a refill when the box went empty. He picked up the box and threw it on the floor in anger. How dare the damn box have the gall to run out? His head suddenly jerked to Mom.

"Get me some more wine," he ordered.

"That was the last," Mom replied while sipping her chicken broth. It was all she could keep down.

Next thing we know Pop slams his fists on the table, stood up and walked to the basement door. The three of us sat there, not touching our food and waiting for the inevitable backlash. Before we moved into the Holler house, I could not fathom a scenario where my Dad would hurt us. He'd spent my entire life protecting us and supporting us. Where do you turn when the one person you're supposed to trust and count on now becomes your tormentor?

Pop opened the door and muttered something about the oil and wine, and the bang of him closing it reverberated off the walls. As he slammed the door we were in for yet another shock. The electric stove's front burner suddenly ignited, and a flame shot a foot off the stovetop. It was an electric stove. How could that happen? We sat there helpless in our fear.

After Mom and Marie cleared the dishes, they went out to do some grocery shopping, and I told them not to forget the damn wine. I was in the living room and got up to get a drink. When I got into the kitchen I faintly heard whispers. Now, whispers were a recent development in the house. I've stated we always felt like we were being watched, but I heard no whispers. I stopped dead at the refrigerator, straining my ears to find the source.

It was coming from the basement.

The door leading to the basement was ancient and hard to keep shut. We installed a hook on the door to keep it closed so the heat would stay upstairs. When Pop slammed the door it hadn't shut completely. I slowly approached the entryway, and the voice got louder.

"No, I can't possibly do that, can I?" it was Pop's voice but in a low tone. I knew I was taking a risk standing there eavesdropping on him, but my curiosity outweighed my fear. He mumbled something I couldn't make out and my skin crawled because of what I was witnessing. The man, who made me and raised me, was not talking to himself as I initially thought. The way he would say something, wait a bit as if he was listening, and then respond showed he was having a conversation with someone... or something.

"Well, you might have a point there," he continued, and he made a sadistic chuckle in agreement with his visitor. My imagination replayed every horror movie I'd ever seen in that moment, and none of them ended well. The knock on the front door brought me out of my shock.

I completely forgot I was going out that night with the guys and Dave picked me up. He came into the kitchen and I was getting my coat on. My expression was not a happy one. Dave was and still is a skeptic in all things supernatural, so I never even bothered to confide in him. But he knew when I was upset.

"You ok bro?" Dave asked.

"Let's just get out of here," I wanted to be far away from the house.

"Pop's down in the cellar? I'm going to go say hello."

I stopped Dave with a hand on his chest.

"Better not," I warned.

"Why not?"

"The old man's got... company." We left the house, and I was glad of it. By that point I was ready to leave the place and my Father with it. If the damn house wanted him so badly, it could have him. Just leave the rest of us alone.

Excerpt from interview with James Hunter:

James: *It was cold out and I didn't want to go out there. He went ballistic and came at me!*

I WAS UP AT THE COLLEGE at yet another alcohol fueled gathering, so I received this story from my siblings the next day. Mostly the house spared James what it was doing to the rest of us, and Pop was not bothering him like the old man came at me. Mainly because he was never home and when he was home, he was in a self-induced Nyquil coma. He didn't want to be conscious in the house. However, on that night he would be the target of our Father's rage. James and Marie were in the living room and Pop was up in his bedroom. The old man came down the steps pissed off as usual.

"Hey, I see a light going off on Joe's car outside. James, head out there and make sure someone's not trying to break in," Pop ordered. He no longer asked.

"Dad, it's cold out there and I'm getting ready to sleep," pleaded James.

Pop's fury went from zero to a hundred as he came at James, screaming with anger about him not listening. James ducked under him and ran out on the porch, trying to comprehend what the hell just happened. The situation escalated even further when Pop stormed out after him. James ran toward the cars as Pop grabbed a shovel off the porch and snapped it over his knee. He chased his son around the cars, threatening him with the broken handle. James needed to run halfway up the driveway to get away from him and after Mom screamed she was calling the police Pop settled down. James stayed outside until Marie came out to get him. To this day, I'm not sure I would've gone back inside after that.

Marie's eyes were welling up as she told me all that had transpired the next day. When Pop went back into the house, Mom noticed the blood pouring out from his hand. He'd sliced his palm open deeply when he broke the shovel.

"Joey you should have been here, he stared at his wound and the blood like he enjoyed it," Marie quivered in fear, "he held it up and said, 'I'm bleeding, there's blood,' and I swear he was laughing at it! What are we going to do?"

"I think we should all look for other places to live. If we keep living here one of us or all of us are going to end up dead."

I wasn't trying to scare her, but it was the way I felt. The house had its claws dug into Pop, and it wasn't letting him go. I shudder to think of what might have happened if Pop had gotten his hands on my brother that night. The torment and terror just seemed to engulf us all. Our family was circling the drain, and the darkness of the abyss seemed to be never ending. We'd only been in the Holler House four months, and we were all but done in by it. Little did we know, there was some light coming our way.

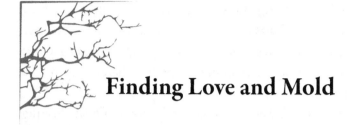

Finding Love and Mold

Excerpt from Interview with Alice Hunter:

Alice: *When I first started dating Joe, he was living in that house. I was only there a few times, but I was never comfortable there. I flat out refused to be alone in the place when I was there. I remember, I never used the bathroom in that house and anyone who knows me knows I can pee anywhere. Not there, though... not in that house. To use the bathroom there would mean I'd have to be alone.*

OUR LAST MONTH IN THE house was fairly quiet compared to the months preceding it. As the spring weather thawed winter's icy grip, my Father's temperament thawed a bit. Mom and Pop began taking walks at night down to Bixby's Lodge, and their relationship was being repaired on those evening strolls. It was on one of those walks Mom convinced him they needed to get out of the house. There was no getting around that decision. Pop agreed, and the two of them started searching for suitable homes for us they could afford.

During this same time of dismal sadness, the universe sent me an angel. I met the woman I would eventually call my wife in the last month in that house. Her name was Alice, and she differed completely from any other girl I'd dated. First off, she was religious. I'm not saying she just believed in a higher power, she lived her life to praise and serve the Lord. In her life, she was serving customers in the department opposite of me at work. I was not very religious and given the events of the past months, if there was a God I had every right to be angry with him. Alice saw something different in me, and for whatever reason, she took a chance on me.

On our first date we went to dinner and after we finished eating, I took her back to my house so we could watch a movie. Yes, I was apprehensive to bring her to the house, but I knew we'd be alone and that was the point. She was not a fan of the place from the start. Once we were inside the house she clung to my side. During the movie I got up to get her a drink and when I closed the fridge in the kitchen, I turned around and she was right behind me. She scared the hell out of me.

Excerpt from interview with Alice Hunter:

Alice: *I gave him some bull story about wanting to be close to him, but it was really the fact I didn't want to be alone for a second. I crossed the foyer from the living room to the kitchen and just glancing up the stairs to the second landing I knew I was being stared at, but there was no one up there.*

A FEW WEEKS PRIOR TO us moving out, Pop obsessed over finding the source of the rotten odor in the bathroom. He thought maybe it was a dead mouse or some other small rodent. He cleaned out the cabinet under the sink and found nothing; the pungent aroma filled his nostrils and turned his stomach. The past few weeks had been slightly better for him. While the dread was still very much there, he could manage it better. He also began apologizing for his mood swings, which was a new and welcoming change of pace.

HOLLER HOUSE

My parents were convinced the various illnesses which I, Marie and Mom herself were suffering from, stemmed from the house. It got so bad; the medical bills were piling up from the emergency room visits. One-night Mom confided in her husband she felt the place was out to kill them, and if it couldn't do so through Pop, it would now try alternative means.

So began the spring cleaning of the Holler House.

From top to bottom, my parents and us three kids scrubbed and washed all we could to rid the place of our ails. My asthma during those breathless months was at an all-time high. I was going through medicine faster than my grandmother could provide. Marie had several bouts of intestinal cramps, vomiting, and diarrhea just like my Mother was going through. So on we scrubbed. We weren't sure it would work, but it was nice to work together toward a common goal as a family.

There Pop stood in the bathroom, unable to produce the source of the odor. It dumbfounded him. He checked all over the bathroom and found no reason for the smell to linger. Just when he was about to call it quits he stepped on one of the many creaky floorboards in the house. The sound of the warped wood beneath his foot made something in his brain click. He kneeled down and with a screwdriver pried up the loose board. It required very minimal effort. At this point in its existence, the house was not fit to live in. To this day, I'm not sure what a housing inspector would have said if we had called one. Joe Hunter Sr was in for an enormous surprise.

Black mold!

The mold spores were so abundant and large you could see them. The horrendous natural intruder ran throughout the entire bathroom. With the removal of one floor board, we solved the mystery of the Hunter sickness. Immediately we knew what was causing all our illnesses. Prolonged exposure to this poison can affect every aspect of a person's body, including the brain, and ultimately lead to permanent damage and the need for a casket. The stuff was a killer.

"June, come up here right now and bring your camera," Pop bellowed down the stairs. "I've got something to show you and we're gonna need pictures."

The mold was the final straw. Once we uncovered it and my parents took several pictures to prove it, my Father called Virginia and there was hell to pay. This was not a recent development. The mold had been there for some time, and that the old woman was still allowing people to live in this house was grounds for neglect.

"Here's the deal Virginia, I'm holding back the last two months' rent so I can move my family somewhere else," Pop was assertive when he spoke to our land Lady.

"You can't do that!" Virginia's shrill voice rang through the receiver, "I'll take you to court, and you signed a six-month lease!"

"Oh, I don't believe you want this case in a courtroom. See, I've got some very interesting pictures of the black mold under my bathroom floor and if I were to make one phone call to the health department, I'm fairly certain a judge would see it my way."

There was an endless pause on the other end of the phone line. For a moment, my Father believed his threats had done the old bird in.

"Fine, just move out by the end of the month, and I want those pictures."

"Oh no, I believe I'll just hang on to them as a memento of our dealings with each other," Pop hung up the phone and his mouth turned in a big wide grin. Possible because he knew he had the money now to find a suitable home for the family.

Excerpt from interview with June Hunter:

June: *Yes, it was far away from all we knew, but we thought after all we'd been through a change in scenery was just what we needed.*

HOLLER HOUSE

A LITTLE MORE THAN a week after Pop informed Virginia we'd be finding new accommodations; they turned my life upside down. For my entire life, they raised me in Pebble Creek or around that area. My father was born and raised in the coal regions of Pa. He loved it up there, and his new route for his business was in and around the areas he grew up and loved as a child.

Mom was searching the local listings along Pop's new route and found one which seemed too good to be true. However, this time she was more cautious, after all the Holler House was just as perfect for us when she found it. She placed a call to the landlord, and he offered to show them the place that very hour.

New Potsdam was a small borough nestled deep in the mountains of School Hill County. When I tell you it was small, I mean small. If you blink you missed this town on the major highway. Yet when Mom and Pop drove to see the house, a sincere feeling of peace came over him. It was the exact opposite of the horrendous dread he'd been suffering from over the last five months. They pulled up and a man around my Father's age was waiting for them. His name was Omar, and he and Pop hit it off from the beginning. When the door opened and Joe Hunter Sr. stepped over the threshold, he put his arm around his wife and said, "I'm home."

Excerpt from interview with Marie Hunter:

Marie: *I didn't care how far away this new place was. I was ready to sleep in a damn cardboard box in it meant getting out of there.*

WHILE MOST OF OUR FAMILY saw it as a joyous occasion for us to be moving out of the Holler house, I considered it bitter sweet. It thrilled me to hear we were getting out of our current, awful situation, but I was not at all happy with where we were moving. New Potsdam was almost fifty miles away from Pebble Creek, and my entire life was there. All of my friends, my job, and now this wonderful girl I'd just met. Everything I knew was in that area, and now I had to leave it all behind. It was not a straightforward process.

Some would say I was a grown adult man who could have moved out on my own, but where the hell was I getting the money? Do you know what the average retail employee makes? Most don't make enough to live on, at least not back then. None of my friends could have me living with them, so I had no choice but to move with my family. The past months had put so much strain and anguish on mine and my father's relationship, I wanted to be as far away from him as possible. We were barely speaking by then. Now here we were moving for the second time in a year and at that point in my young, irresponsible mind it was *his* fault.

Once the family decided that we were moving it appeared whatever was troubling Pop no longer held much sway over him. He became obsessed with getting his family out of that house as soon as possible and up north where we could start fresh. Looking back now, as a father myself, I see how much of a child I was to blame him. I also regret my attitude in the weeks leading up to the move. I wasn't happy about leaving, and it sure as hell was no secret.

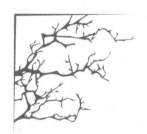

Moving Day

Excerpt from interview with Joe Hunter Sr., June Hunter, and Marie Hunter:

Joe: *I was so happy we were getting out of there. When I woke up that morning I couldn't wait to get the truck and leave that wretched place behind us.*

June: *In my lifetime I've moved a lot and I cannot remember when I packed and was ready to leave quicker than when I packed to leave that house.*

Marie: *I kept waiting for the horror movie ending. You know, when everything is going great, and it looks like all is well, and then a hand reaches out and pulls you back into the nightmare. That's what it was like that last day.*

Excerpt from interview with Alice Hunter:

Alice: *It shocked me when Joe told me he was moving all the way up there. We just started dating and now he's moving away! I figured that was it for us.*

THE SUN WAS SHINING on that warm spring day in May. Pop commented it was an omen of good fortune considering we moved into the place in hellish weather, and now the weather was perfect when we were leaving. My brother and I couldn't get the day off so we had to work till that afternoon and by the time we got to the Holler House our friends and family were setting a record pace.

The U-Haul was already half way loaded up, and they already packed the beds and couches up. Most of the heavy stuff was ready to go, and now everyone was concentrating on the smaller items. When James and I pulled up Pop was acting as supervisor and directing everyone. I remember he really didn't go back into the place while we were moving out. To this day, I don't know if that was a conscious decision or instinct.

"Good, you boys are finally here," Pop wasn't happy we had to work that day.

"I couldn't call out Pop, I need the money," I shot back with venom in my voice, "It's going to cost me a lot in gas money to keep making the trip back down here."

Pop's eyes narrowed as my words stung him. It was just another jab, reminding him I didn't want to move to New Potsdam.

"We need to get the dressers off the top floors, get up there and help Dave and Mike," Pop ordered.

With the extra man power our friends provided, we could get the house empty in record time. Mike, Dave and Allen were and still are to this day some of the best people I've ever met. Allen was actually the younger brother of one of our other friends, but he and James were in school together. They really came through for us when it mattered, and I believe I still owe Dave a moving favor or two.

The last big thing we needed to get out was the washer from the basement, and it wasn't easy at all. It was big and awkward and required two people just to get it up the steps and into the truck. We got the damn thing stuck so many times it was as if something didn't want us to leave. Dave and I had it cockeyed in the basement doorway, and I called for Mike to come down and give us a hand. Unbeknownst to me, Mike was upstairs with Marie on the third floor cleaning out the last dresser. She asked him to go up there with her for obvious reasons.

We made it a point that day not to let anyone alone in the house for any reason. There was safety in numbers and we wanted to leave the house with the same number of people. My friends didn't really buy into the paranormal events in the house, so when I called for Mike to come help us out he didn't see an issue leaving Marie up on the third floor by herself.

Within moments of being alone in James' bedroom, Marie could feel the chill enter the room. She was up there feeding the cable down through the third-floor window to Pop, who was outside. Pop didn't want to leave it behind. As she fed the last bit out the window, she heard this sudden, loud *bang* behind her. Marie spun and to her horror she saw one of the dresser drawers was lying against the wall on the other side of the room. Before she reacted another of the heavy drawers launched itself across the room!

"Oh my God!" Marie shouted. Her scream was loud enough to alert Allen, who was down on the second floor. He came barreling up the stairs to make sure she was ok. Back then Allen and I were not very close but I am proud to say today he has made my sister Marie and their two children happy. He is still protecting her as he did that day.

"What's wrong?" he asked.

"We have to hurry," she replied, and the two of them stacked the drawers and proceeded down the steps as fast as they could. When they got to the second floor landing Marie caught sight of our Grandfather's crucifix hanging on the wall. Her eyes bulged with terror as the holy relic turned itself upside down, almost mocking what it represented. She shook her head and in a moment of unthinkable bravery grabbed the cross off the wall and headed out to the moving truck.

By that time, we had the washer loaded up and Dave and Allen went back up for the last dresser. Mike and I went back up to the third floor, just to take another look at my poker room. It was a damn shame we didn't get to enjoy our hard work more so than we did. I don't have a lot of pleasant memories from that house, but most of them revolve around the guys and me building that room.

"Sorry you wasted your time, Mike," I said, running my hands across the red walls.

"I don't consider it a waste bro, we had fun doing it," Mike answered back. Certain events would lead to a falling out with him a few years later, but even when he wasn't a part of my life, I still held fond memories of him.

EXCERPT FROM INTERVIEW with June Hunter:

June: *It was as if she had to get one last scare in before we left.*

WITH THE TRUCK LOADED and the sun was setting over Pebble Creek. Pop and the boys started heading up north to our new home to move into the new place. Mom and Marie were going to stay and clean up for an hour. By then Zack would be there and he would bring them to New Potsdam. We were not happy about leaving them, but they said they would be fine and they would stay on the first floor. So reluctantly we left them at the house to clean.

The two women were laughing and joking while they straightened up the house. Mom didn't want to leave Virginia for any reason to come after us. She was finished with this place once and for all. They were losing light rapidly when Mom was finishing vacuuming the downstairs. As she began vacuuming the stairs, she felt the *eyes* on her again. She quickly glanced up and there was Mary Mack again, glaring down at her with even more hatred and contempt. She froze for only a second.

"Marie, get your stuff and get out on the porch *now*," Mom ordered. She confided in me later that was when she felt the most threatened. If this entity was going to make its last stand, it would be then.

"I'm almost done in here, Mom..." She stepped next to Mom and her words escaped her. The slightest whimper left her throat.

"Get out on the porch right now!" Mom bellowed. Her daughter didn't say another word and rushed through the front door. June wasted no time grabbing her vacuum and following her out. When they were outside Mom went to turn and shut the door and let out a fearful yelp.

There she was, face to face with the entity, with only a thin screen door separating them. Mom was staring in the face of evil as she gawked into the old woman's black eyes. "You can have the house bitch, but I'm taking my family," and Mom and Marie walked out on the bridge to wait for Zack. Not one of us set foot in that place ever again.

Harboring Resentment
and a Cleansing Fire

Excerpt from interview with Joe Hunter Sr.:

Joe: *The two of us were at each other's throats. My son was constantly picking fights with me, and my temper and pride couldn't abide it.*

POP IMMEDIATELY SET about making the new house a home. From day one in that place, he started hanging pictures and giving the place details here and there to add that Hunter charm. I wanted no part of the new town and absolutely no part of him. After all the horrible fights and constant belittling of me, I'd grown to hate the man. My siblings and my Mother were perfectly content with just putting everything behind them, but I just couldn't. It has always been a Hunter weakness to hold grudges. My dad would be the first one to tell you that. Mom and Dad have been living up in New Potsdam for fifteen years now; I was there for less than one of them.

I would constantly undermine Pop every chance I got and every time he'd attempt to have us, as a family, enjoy our new town, I'd blow him off. I really was being a complete jerk to him and the rest of my family. Even though I knew it wasn't my father's fault and he had no control over the situation, I couldn't forgive him.

The next Christmas Alice and I got engaged and a few months later Pop and I had our final blow up at each other. It was a very nasty fight which culminated in Pop grabbing a picture off the wall and slamming it over my head. To his credit, he'd made sure it was a picture without glass in it. My mother told me it was time for me to find a place of my own, and I packed up my car and moved out.

For several months I lived a nomadic existence. I would stay at a friend's house till they grew tired of me and then I would move on. Eventually I lived with my grandmother for a few weeks until Alice and I found the money to move into our own apartment. It was rough for a while; Pop and I still weren't speaking. This went on for several months, almost to where I figured he wouldn't be at my wedding. Sometimes I'd think back on Miss Mary Mack and think to myself, *she won, she tore us apart*, now I realize it was just me not being able to forgive Pop.

It took some doing and some badgering from Mom, Marie, and Alice, but finally we two stubborn, hard-headed men put our differences aside and reconnected. Pop apologized for everything that happened in that house. Marie brought him up to speed because he could barely remember the months we lived in the Holler House. To him it was all a blur after he received that post card from Sloan. I accepted his apology and the two of us began rebuilding our relationship. It wasn't easy at first, but we found our stride. I'm very glad the two of us made amends because I can't imagine a life where Pop Hunter never gets to hug his grandchildren. Just watching their eyes light up when they see Pop Pop and Nanny is proof enough that Mary Mack didn't win.

EXCERPT FROM INTERVIEW with James Hunter:

HOLLER HOUSE

James: *I was in the Army by that point and stationed in Hawaii, I was lying in bed and my best friend messaged me and told me, 'THE HOUSE FROM HELL IS ON FIRE!'*

JAMES CALLED ME IN a frantic state. He was almost out of breath as he spoke to me. It was completely out of the ordinary to get a call from him. He'd spent fourteen months in Afghanistan and was now a Staff Sergeant. Over the years, he and I had grown further and further apart. He was serving his country, and I was raising a family.

"Bro, did you hear the news?!" James gasped.

"Slow down, what happened?" I asked.

"There was a fire at the old house, the place burned to the ground!"

I nearly dropped my phone. The memories came rushing back, the house, the fear, the entity. In an instant I was back in my poker room setting up a game and there she was standing in the doorway again.

"The Holler House," my voice was not much more than a whisper.

According to the local papers, the authorities deemed the house unfit for human beings and condemned a few years prior and they sold the property. Virginia moved to a nursing home and spent her remaining days there. She died in 2018 at ninety, proving no matter how much money a person has, death is the great equalizer. After interviewing several of her nurses, one of them finally offered an interesting story. In the last days of Virginia's life, she would cry out in the middle of the night, "She's coming, she's coming!" and on the night before her heart gave out, "She's here... she's here!"

It makes you wonder if the house wanted one last victim for itself.

As for the fire, no one is certain what happened to the place. We know that one cold winter night, the Holler House ignited mysteriously and although the fire fighters did their jobs well, they couldn't save the place. Rumors circulated that some of them swear they heard ungodly screams as the flames engulfed the structure. I could confirm none of those. They didn't find anyone in the house once they extinguished the flames.

The next year, the new owner realized there was no salvaging the historic site, and had the entire structure torn down. All that sits now is a vacant lot, and there is no access from the main road anymore. However, I'm sure that doesn't stop curious teens from venturing down toward the spot where such evil dwelled. After reading the news about the house's ultimate demise, I felt a sense of closure. It felt like I could let go of all those painful memories. Still, there are some thoughts too difficult to shake.

Final Thoughts

Excerpt from interview with Joe Hunter Sr.:

Joe: *Good riddance to that damn place. I'm home now. That place was never a home. I just wish I could remember... why can't I remember?*

Excerpt from interview with June Hunter:

June: *It was a relief, like a weight lifted off my shoulders, because I truly felt my husband was going to take my life and my children's. It's a mother's worst fear thinking of something like that happening to your babies.*

Excerpt from interview with Marie Hunter:

Marie: *It was all the proof I need to know evil walks among us and can attack you from any angle. I never feared before and haven't feared my father since that house. There was something in that house you couldn't explain.*

Excerpt from interview with James Hunter:

James: *When I received news the place burned down, I felt an incredible relief and peace. That house was born out of hell and its unfortunate we had to live there, but if there was one positive spin you can put on it; we came out of it stronger.*

I REALIZE THERE ARE some who will read this and claim it never happened. I understand it takes an open mind and no small amount of faith to believe the events in this story occurred, but they did. I also did some digging into the effects of black mold on the human system. While the illnesses we experienced in the house were probably the result of exposure to the mold, some other events are harder to explain away. To be honest, I don't care whether people think this story is true of a work of fiction. I know in my heart what happened and my family knows it. Writing this, and reliving all these memories, has provided me with a therapeutic outlet. It is a good thing.

My own thoughts on the matter are: In this world you need to fight for what you believe in, and my family was in the fight of their lives for those five months. Evil exists, and we experienced it. The overall power of the entity in that God forsaken house was so palpable and so malevolent; we barely escaped as a family. Evil wasn't the only thing proven to exist in that hellhole. It ultimately proved to me that love and sheer will to survive can in fact triumph over evil. When we received the news, the place had burned to the ground I had one very clear thought. Was it in fact over? Did the evil which dwelt in Holler House return to the hell it belonged to? Whenever I drive past that old empty lot I still get a shiver up my spine, remembering my experience, the terror, and the horror we endured at Holler House.

THE END

About the Author

Mark Kurtis Jr was born and raised in eastern Pennsylvania. He still resides in the Keystone State with his loving wife and two energetic children. He has been a storyteller since he was able to speak, and writing stories since he was able to hold a crayon.

His debut novel, Child of Magic, was originally meant as a birthday present for his wife. After much convincing, she urged him to share it with the world.

Mark is an avid reader, a huge movie buff, and draws his inspiration from all avenues of his life.